APPETITE
FOR
RISK

APPETITE
FOR
RISK

What It Is, Who Has It
& How I Survived

— AN ADVENTURE MEMOIR —

Robert R. Abbott

REGENT PRESS
Berkeley, California

[paperback]
ISBN 13: 978-1-58790-654-1
ISBN 10: 1-58790-654-6

[e-book]
ISBN 13: 978-1-58790-655-8
ISBN 10: 1-58790-655-4

Library of Congresss Control Number: 2023022172

Cover art and design by Priscila Soares

Interior layout and design by Mark Weiman

MANUFACTURED IN THE U.S.A.
REGENT PRESS
Berkeley, California
www.regentpress.net

Contents

THIS BOOK IS DEDICATED

TO MY CHILDREN, TOM AND MICHELLE,

AND THEIR MOTHER, CYNTHIA.

WHAT A JOY IT HAS BEEN, EVERY BIT OF IT!

Author's Note

THE BIG BLACK REVOLVER was inches from my forehead. I was absolutely calm, and eventually the man I later found out was on the FBI's Most Wanted list put away the gun. Years earlier, while I was serving in the Peace Corps, a crew of river pirates had crashed my canoe into the tangled mangrove roots of a narrow channel in Nigeria. They brandished machetes and without knowing why, I shouted out words in a strange language. They froze. From *words*!

Like many kids of Irish descent, I inherited the gift of gab, or so I'd been assured by my mother, who had a wild past herself. Maybe my Hibernian ancestors had a way with words too—and were spared from the atrocities of the English because of it. Regardless, thanks to a wealth of time on my hands due to a global pandemic, I am now using words to relive a slew of adventures, many of them in my twenties and thirties. Familiar markers appear in the form of phrases perfected in bars, mansions, grass huts, and at boat docks around the globe as I have told and retold these amazing stories of my real life experiences.

And yes, at my age, memories recede, stories conflate. Thankfully, some of them live on in relics on my shelves and walls, letters to my parents, and old photographs. Surprisingly, most of my "highlight reels" have not faded, probably because intense emotions burned them deep into my memory banks. Intense emotions which, added to reflection, are now pinned to these pages, hopefully without losing all vestiges of voice inflection and hand gestures.

In what follows, you will meet the gunman on the Most Wanted List, the river pirates, deadly snakes, and more, as they encountered a testosterone-driven bonehead adrenaline addict—who eventually grew up, but without abandoning risky pursuits. Along the way there was a disastrous Hawaiian romance, which saw me fall head over heels, blow it, and hit bottom, before rebounding, starting a family, and pursuing a career in marine biology that took me to even farther flung locales.

Parts of my past still make me pause and clear my throat. My hands trembled when I set out to relate one specific near-death experience. Silently, again and again I thank the angels in human form who somehow appeared in time to pull my fat-headed bacon out of the fire.

Intermixed with escapades you will find a theory that has been knocking around in my head for decades. It consists of three-pronged speculations: on genetic drivers, the influence of upbringing, and my evolution into a mystic (even as I continued to adhere to the primacy of science). It all ties together. Trust me.

Before shifting into the stories that put the flesh on the bones of those theories, I think it is proper to introduce myself. My given name is Robert. Neither Robert nor Bob was a good fit, and Bud is the name I have chosen, the name everyone now calls me. In my mind, it is linked to the idea of growth and potential in a flower not yet opened.

Did My Ancestors Make Me Do It?

DEATH REPEATEDLY KNOCKS on my door. I politely decline to exercise that option. Even so, at eighty-two, daily I am unencumbering physical elements of my life. My time will come. But afterward, maybe others will chance upon these words and meet a guy with an appetite for risk who kept coming up smelling like a rose and asking why, and just maybe gained some insights on the whys and ways of being in the world, and of raising a family in a potentially treacherous changing world.

What, then, *is* the appetite for risk, and who has it? Like the appetite for a piece of dark chocolate, risk in its varying expressions is alluring, and its taste is savory, dopamine-triggering, life-affirming, delicious. We all have the capacity for this appetite, but some are more prone to it than others. Consider for a moment the possibility that serial risk-takers are the Life Force's exploratory fringe, and that much of the success of the naked ape is attributable to the outliers who crossed the big river teeming with crocodiles, explored an adjacent beach or the valley just over the hills, faced off against large predators, and confronted a different band of hunter-gatherers to push at the edge of the environment for nutrition, shelter, and mates from other gene pools. This small percentage of the human population is less guided by fear and more driven to see a challenge as a rollicking, good opportunity.

My life has taken me all over the globe, as far as Western China. All animals have migratory drives, and for better and worse, we are situated on the continuum of animals. Waves of Huns, Visigoths, and Mongol invaders from the East precede us, and surely that genetic drive, I'm convinced, is in my genome. It could be in yours too.

I have long sought an explanation for my behaviors, on the one hand in terms of DNA. But while I am a trained scientist, I am not a pure materialist. My parallel identity as an explorer of the ineffable transcendent elements within and around us also informs my outlook, one that goes well beyond a "my genes made me do it" mentality. Sure, many of my peer-review-driven colleagues will consider my forays into psychic phenomena such as Controlled Remote Viewing and astral travel a gateway to residence in a rubber room. They are entitled to their opinion! But my experiences are very real to me.

❏ ❐ ❏

Through the prism of science, I stand on the shoulders of giants, evolutionary biologists who have established that the lineage of all living things is based on an organic chemical, or better put, a biochemical life form whose characteristic is to survive and reproduce. Reproduce yes, but innovate, adapt, or cease to exist!

Gambling comes into the picture too. To gamble for something of value is virtually universal, whether for money, renown, power, or sex/love. At times with amusement, at times with chagrin, I can now see the young, cocksure version of myself clearly trying to hog attention or get the eye of a lady. I still remember doing a double leg sweep over the second story rail at Point Loma High School—to catch the attention of my high school sweetheart Donna.

But there is more than rampant testosterone to grapple with. *Something* compelled me early on and does to this day. But *what?* Restlessness? Curiosity? An exceptionally robust suite of early childhood experiences, supported by a nurturing family? Audacity? Fearlessness in the decisive moment?

All of the above adds up to what I have identified as the APPETITE FOR RISK.

❏ ❐ ❏

Wordsworth said the child is the father of the man, and my own background is on the surface all-American, carrying attendant privileges: a WASP upbringing in a supportive family post-WWII. At the age of twelve, I walked onto the stage at a Billy Graham revival meeting and was "saved"—very temporarily. After an extended university career that took me to Mexico, Chile, Switzerland, and various locales domestically, I joined the Peace Corps and was posted to Nigeria. After more bouncing around, I earned a PhD in marine biology, a field that took me to over fifty-five countries and five continents. A marine biologist is at home wherever there are bodies of water, and as most grade school children know but many adults forget, the Earth is over 70 percent water.

❏ ❐ ❏

On one level, I may need to tell my stories one last time before I let them go. But there are other levels, in the realms of cultural anthropology, neuro-physiology, and metaphysics. And beyond those levels, there is still another one, more primeval and personal.

It goes back to early childhood. I recently found a photo of myself at age five or six that confirmed a memory of standing in a wooden planter box. I was holding a spear. I also remember crossing an imaginary river in Alaska as an imaginary companion to Jack London's White Fang, an experience that was remanifested decades later when my dugout canoe was beset by river pirates. Growing up in an urban farm environment foreshadows countless near fatal mishaps with animals and guns. And the circuitous link between my Uncle Tom's PT boat missions in the Pacific Theater and my encounters with trigger-happy men in uniforms is hard to miss. The connections go on.

A snapshot of me in the family swing set foreshadowed later scenes of skydiving, surfing, and cliff diving in La Jolla. Reaching further back, I discern a faint but unmistakable trail between my great-grandparents crossing and re-crossing North America and my own perilous confrontations with Indigenous People, in my incarnation as a representative of a cultural invasion in conflict with Native Hawaiians. All of the above no doubt played into my so easily falling into the web of a criminal underclass—all Caucasian—in Hawaii.

❑ ❐ ❑

To be clear, I am not a proponent of pathological risk-taking as described in the DCM-IV, nor am I a compulsive gambler or substance abuser. And while more than once I've been informed, "My husband has a gun," rest assured that this is not a collection of salacious sexual experiences populating my libido.

On the subject of sex, it is factual that our genetic code is 98 percent the same as the bonobo chimpanzee. The sexiest mammal on the planet, bonobos have sex anytime one feels good, is scared, or finds something to eat. Find food. Get it on. Drink water, get it on. Early morning, get it on. Fieldwork on bonobos has given us a better understanding of human behaviors and proclivities.

Bonobos notwithstanding, late in life I've come to realize how unthinking and naïve I had been on the man-woman thing. My early behavior patterns, confronted unflinchingly, are retold in these pages, and not with pride. Toxic masculinity is real, and I have made amends as I can.

Going forward entails looking back, and coming to terms with our fellow primates and ancestors. Hunter-gatherers wandered across Africa, the Middle East, and Asia as small groups or tribes. From the Trojan War to the Vikings, from Pacific Islanders to the Inca Empire and the Yanomamö Indians, the willingness of men to kill each other to gain access to women who will pass on their genes has been abundantly documented. Alexander the Great once demanded that a city send out all its women or his army would kill all the men and children. The city sent out its women. Such is history, politically correct or not. Our history—yours and mine. Acknowledging it without value judgement is integral to my development, and the development of our species. (I am a non-dual reality guy. It just makes more sense.) The ones that took risks and survived are the forebears of us all.

❏ ❐ ❏

The ancestral energy field that predisposes me to encounter danger—my appetite for risk, and propensity for survival—apparently remains intact. As recently as a 2021 trip to Costa Rica to select a site for a spiritual retreat, the first of several in the works, my travel partner and I encountered a once-in-a-century rainfall and an earthquake. Making our way out was hair-raising, but we got through it.

That's me, always becoming, yet in some ways still as I was. Like a kid, playing beside a mud puddle, pounding kitchen pots and pans, who does not want to come home for dinner, I do not

want to curtail my inclinations because I have been dealt a terrific hand by fate. It would be inappropriate not to play out that
hand with gusto.

1.
PILGRIMAGE TO GALÁPAGOS

*"A man who dares to waste one hour of time
has not discovered the value of life."*
— CHARLES DARWIN

Pre-pandemic, I found myself in conversation with a bust on a low pedestal. It was hot, and I was tired after a long walk around Isla Santa Cruz in Ecuador, but the Great Elucidator—who had articulated evolution, a process that like magnetism cannot be known except by its effects on the material world—refused to be ignored. Approaching the likeness, I bent at the waist and stretched out my arms, then with deep veneration bowed, saying, "I hail you, Charles Darwin. You saw the pieces of the puzzle and tied them all together to reveal the majesty of the force for perpetual change." At the base of the small statue were dried flowers and seashells scattered by others also paying their homage.

I was in the presence of the Master, having a religious experience as profound to me as a Muslim pilgrim's walk around the Kaaba in Saudi Arabia, or a devout Christian's visit to Golgotha in Israel. The state of mind during a spiritual experience is like a rush of serotonin, endorphins, dopamine, and oxytocin hormones through your whole body at the same time. But it passed quickly, and I still had to register for two days of dive trips, along with my travel companion, Christiana. At seventy-eight I was on the road again, like Willie Nelson. Willie is older than me but still out there doing his thing the world over, and his theme song fits me to a T.

Across from the statue, at the Iguana Dive Shop, which calls itself "the undisputed leader in Galápagos diving," I showed my Advanced Open Water scuba diving card, earned on a four-day "live aboard" dive trip in Thailand a few years earlier, which had really tested my mettle. There were three dives a day at sites in the Andaman Sea. I did OK but by the third day I took only two dives, and by the fourth was exhausted, taking only the last dive at a boat wreck in shallow water.

For this trip, I had trained hard at various pools, then with a few short swims in the San Francisco Bay. My fascination with scuba diving went back to watching *The Undersea World of Jacques Cousteau* as a child. Later, completing my marine biology degree, I dove for black abalone and in a study of harbor seals in the brutally cold Puget Sound. Wherever I'd traveled, I tried to get in some diving, including at a geologic fault zone in Iceland, off the tiny Pacific Island of Tuvalu, and in China, Taiwan, Oman, and Indonesia (Sulawesi and Borneo).

At the Iguana Dive Shop, they wanted more documentation, and I produced a letter from my doctor attesting to my good health, before signing a thorough injury disclaimer. Christiana and I were in Ecuador to take two dives daily near some remote rocky islets, former volcanos that make up the Galápagos Islands.

The long, pounding boat trips to the Seymour Channel and Bartolomé Island proved to be a challenge, but this old guy was game, and so was Christiana, despite rides to the dive sites that made her seasick. Even in the water after exiting the boat she suffered, and small fish feasted on her vomit as she struggled on the surface. But once underwater she was good to go. She particularly appreciated the sea lions that would follow us down to the bottom to snatch up small fish and shrimp stirred up by the eddies and the swirls of our fins.

Christiana is of Vietnamese-American extraction. We had met over a decade ago, after the end of my first marriage. Traveling with a female friend platonically was fairly new to me, a leading indicator of my evolving attitude and behavior. My offering her this opportunity, expenses paid, was a gesture of appreciation; our friendship had grown out of a business relationship—as a real estate finance professional, she found the mortgage money for this marginally employed senior to buy several condos that had appreciated substantially. There was also my very practical need for a companion who would know what to do with the body if I died.

She turned out to be a boon companion. Lots of energy and curiosity. We stayed on three different islands and together enjoyed the wildlife right on the sidewalks in the main towns. Sea lions would waddle up the boat ramps and press into the crowds of people near the boat landing. Fat marine iguanas camped out anywhere they liked, to warm in the sun to speed up digestion before returning to the rocky coast to feed on submerged sea weeds. One of our best days was snorkeling in lava tubes with nocturnal sharks and giant sea turtles.

Yes, some of the long boat rides were jarringly uncomfortable and wet, but the destinations always proved spectacular. Our day trip to the Charles Darwin Research Station dedicated to breeding the variety of giant tortoises specific to each island was a highlight. And long walks through brush-tangled wilds to remote beaches were like magic. Even for a trained marine biologist, it was hard to imagine how giant tortoises could make their way from lush vegetated highlands to sandy beaches to lay their eggs, given these expanses of convoluted volcanic rock and dense, vine-tangled brush. Amazing! We had a blast.

Five days prior, traveling alone, I had been hospitalized in Peru with *Blastocystis hominis*, a severe gastrointestinal infection that started midday as I walked toward a music store to buy a Peruvian guitar. Feeling lightheaded, I stepped into a small tourist restaurant and collapsed at a corner table. I got sicker by the minute and asked for a "Bote de Basra." The waiter brought a plastic bag and I heaved into it. My head hit the table. I could barely lift it up to ask for help. Long minutes later a team of short, stout men got their shoulders under my arms and dragged me out with my legs waving uncontrollably like the floppy animated blow-up figures you see on the roofs of tire stores to attract customers. At a Swiss-related hospital, I was given a bed, but only after they confirmed I had a valid credit card and medical insurance—all this as I lay semi-comatose on a dolly in a hallway.

After twenty-four hours on drip antibiotics, I was told they needed the bed for the survivors of a horrific automobile accident. My discharge was predicated solely on my ability to stand up, if slowly, and balance unsteadily by the hospital bed without support. Twenty minutes later I was pushed into a taxicab with a handful of papers and a package of pills. After a wretched night's sleep, I caught a plane from Cuzco to Lima and spent most of two days in bed. The third day I felt better. Then it was off to Quito to meet up with Christiana and fly to the Galápagos. I should have had a travel companion in Peru but was still in "macho man mode," complete with the "I don't need no stinking help" mentality that goes along with it.

❑ ❐ ❑

According to Darwin, as well as Freud and company, thirst

for sheer power is a driving force for many men. Alpha males have it in their genes to seek diverse outlets for their sexual drive, which has precipitated mass death and destruction, to the cost of our human family. Though I do not see much of the drive for power in myself, I have had the honor of meeting several heads of state, including Gerald Ford when I was working in the Sultanate of Oman. At an official reception we chatted about lantern fish in the Indian Ocean. He seemed to like me and afterward I was notified to contact him if I wanted a federal job.

Of course, President Ford was surrounded by men and women with machine guns. One of the men always raked the room with an absolutely fearsome look, regarding everyone as a potential threat. He had a deep depression in his forehead and a long jawline. "That man can kill and probably has, more than once" went through my head every time I saw him.

I also met the President of the Republic of Kiribati, at a frolicking party with dancers and drummers. His protection detail stayed busy intercepting drunks, who staggered around the big community house hoping that in exchange for their votes, the president would *babusi* (gift) them a drink.

Even in the relative safety of the Galápagos, the specter of the unbridled alpha male on the prowl found me, when on the way to a dive site Christiana and I ended up with three Russians. Two of them were tall and broad shouldered, and the other was smaller than average, with a nearly bald head. I sat with them on the boat for an hour. The small man was exceptionally secretive, staying in toilets at transition points and on the boat. He barely spoke, saying only that he was from London and worked in real estate. The tall men were not talkative either. In time I took them to be his bodyguards. To me, the small, bald man looked a *lot* like still another head of state: Vladimir Putin. Christiana saw the resemblance but pointed out that he looked younger than Putin. Maybe a relative? But I still wonder: Why the obvious bodyguards and who, really, was he?

Scuba diving did not take up all my time in the Galápagos, however. The proximity to Darwin's old stomping grounds led me to think more deeply about the nature of risk. Genetics from Darwin to Mendel through the present cuts to the heart of the matter. My family genealogy, worked out by my sister Susanna, makes it clear that I am of North European stock, with a lot of English, Irish, and Scot mixed in, followed by on the order of ten generations migrating to and crisscrossing North America. The implications are of predominantly Anglo-Saxon conquerors.

Preliminary findings suggest that DNA sequences predispose a person's fear response. My assertion is that a paucity of the sequences related to fear among my ancestors, coupled with my upbringing, provided me with robust problem-solving skills. The combination both put me in a host of potentially lethal—as in deader than a doornail—situations and allowed me to survive them. Like a ten-year-old plunging into the pounding surf, I just lurched ahead well into my thirties and to some extent to this very day.

❏ ❐ ❏

My reconnection with Charles Darwin in the Galápagos marked a huge turning point in my life. Although Darwin's contributions tend to be viewed through an exclusively secular lens, he has also helped open humanity up to thinking about forces that cannot be seen. You cannot see "evolution," you can only see the effects of the process. Which takes me to the subject of the unseen world as I have experienced it.

Despite the fact that at times my drives can seem unnervingly instinctual, maddeningly similar to those of birds migrating north in the spring, and monarch butterflies with epigenetic memory of where their forbears mated, my own wavelength has been increasingly tuned toward the spiritual—which is where I diverge from Darwin, the Master.

I doubt he would have embraced the variety of mystical traditions that infuse my views about behavior, including (as mentioned earlier) Controlled Remote Viewing (now routinely taught to military intelligence specialists) and astral travel, along with a belief that free will comes into play once you are able to see the events of the world without setting values or making judgments. Overall, I have come to view our species as a life form for advanced civilizations of curious observers (UFOs) to study—much as I took part in a research projects on fish in lakes and the ocean, and hyenas in South Africa. Which leads me to believe that we quite possibly know as little about reality as a huge colony of African termites know about their ecological relationship to elephants.

So much for the speculations. Now, on to a guided tour through my younger lives, chock-full of nail-biters and the presumed immortality of youth.

2.
SEVENTEENTH JUMP IN AN OLD CARGO CHUTE

*"Skydiving is like cutting your throat and seeing
if you can get to the doctor before you bleed to death."*
— BROCK YATES

Nearly **sixty years earlier,** on September 6, 1962, legally an adult, if barely, I made a series of small mistakes that cumulatively almost killed me. To use a non-technical term, it was a colossal clusterfuck. In the language of skydiving, I experienced a Mae West, with additional complications.

When you jump out of a plane and fall from zero to terminal velocity at 174 feet per second in twelve seconds, there is no room for error. The wind surges past your face and the ground rushes up at a disastrous, teeth-clenching rate—all of it in seeming slow-motion. In a well-managed dive, at terminal velocity you need to be in a sort of birdlike position, arms spread wide, legs apart, your body more or less horizontal, to reduce falling speed and extend the time to do tricks. And if you start at 4,600 feet, you need to open your parachute at about 2,000 feet, or within fifteen seconds of free fall. You'll generally only have a matter of seconds to pop the chute. Too soon and the wind may carry you away from the marked landing zone. Too late and that's all she wrote.

My wiser, younger brother Greg has a saying: "Before a major disaster, fourteen things go wrong." By the time my parachute malfunctioned, I had lost count. Overconfidence and carelessness—common enough in twenty-year-old males—made for an unholy combination: I was falling at 120 mph and everything happened ruthlessly fast, putting me on a collision course with rocky, rusty yellow Southern California terra firma, hard enough to break most of the bones in my body and leave my internal organs splayed out around me.

❑ ❐ ❑

The preamble to this early brush with death took place in Geneva the summer before, which was a real eye-opener for a naïve surfer kid from Southern California. I wanted to be a diplomat and save the world, which seemed to need a lot of saving, with the Cold War in full swing and the US and Russia playing a game of nuclear chicken. There were foreign wars of conquest and liberation. Somebody had to do something, and an International Institutions program at the University of Geneva in historically neutral Switzerland seemed like the place to be.

I had won a scholarship by knowing the difference between the British parliamentary system and the three-pronged division of American government, and by displaying a sense of humor about many things I did not know. The other students were mostly older, the children of diplomats or international conglomerates, and many were the multilingual products of international boarding schools. They radiated a wealth and sophistication that left me feeling diminished and insignificant.

Heated classroom debates as we listened on earphones to lectures in one of five languages left me in a haze of confusion, but the third floor *pension* where I had meals with a potpourri of students and business people, including a hefty Russian woman who worked for the USSR Ministry of Trade and Commerce, was a sanctuary. More importantly, I met Guanella, a pretty Swedish girl fluent in all five languages used in the lectures. She was training to be a simultaneous translator.

Guanella and I hung out in the little restaurants and coffee shops near Lake Geneva. One morning we were sitting at a sidewalk café sipping small cups of strong coffee when I picked up a copy of the *International Herald Tribune* and read about a skydiving accident. The debonair Greek man having coffee with us explained an unfamiliar skydiving term—"Mae West"—using his hands cupped at his chest and alluding to the American movie actress known for her exceptional endowment. The term referred to the extra-large brassiere required to support her amplitude.

Apparently, when one of the parachute cords becomes tangled over the chute and divides it into two smaller sections, a parachute looks much like such a gigantic bra, at which point fatality is imminent. The victim whose death was reported in the paper hit the ground at about a hundred mph when the main chute collapsed, creating a streamer. The debonair Greek also spoke of a student he'd known at the Sorbonne killed from the same type of malfunction.

From that moment I was locked in on the idea of skydiving. The part about being killed had no effect on me. None. Instead, to impress Guanella, I broadcast my willingness to skydive, given the chance. Little did I know that I was only months away from my own Mae West malfunction.

❏ ❑ ❏

Soon after, I returned to San Diego on a passenger ship out of Rotterdam with about a thousand college students. Now that was a party! Back home, thumbing through the Yellow Pages I found a group of sport skydivers who met in a WWII-era ragged greenish building adjacent to a small private airport near Miramar, close to where I was attending college. Driving there, I came upon a small office with some open space, a blackboard, and two long parachute packing tables. When asked my age, I was vague, to avoid the need for permission from my parents. I was one year shy of legal adulthood.

The trainer was about thirty and had a cast on his left arm. He talked to a small group of us about a "hard landings," but did not elaborate. From there, he got right into the nuts and bolts, precisely detailing the parts of a parachute, including the open panels and control lines for steering.

Somehow, Mom found out what I was doing and insisted that I set up a mutual fund account to cover funeral costs! I had to put 10 percent of my earnings from my part-time job at the airport into the fund; doing so taught me about investing and money management, which is sort of funny given that I was supposedly saving up to pay for my own funeral.

I enrolled in the skydiving class, where I learned to jump off stands at various heights. Before, during, and after class the guys told airplane and jump stories; cross-talk covered different types of parachutes, freefall tricks, and accidents.

The ground in front of the building, where we were taught to jump and roll had been dug up and loosened to make practice landing easier on the knees and ankles. Piece of cake. I had been doing gymnastics for years: roundoffs, back handsprings, backflips, and more.

None of my friends were the least bit interested in skydiving. Even my younger brother Greg, who was generally up for anything, declined. Surfing was his passion: long boards and girls in skimpy swimsuits were of much more interest to him. But once, a young woman I knew from the university joined me to train. I was stoked, imagining her as my girlfriend. We would skydive together! But she could not deal with the jump from the highest stand and never came back. In 1962, the skydiving club was a male bastion. (Women were club support and wives and girlfriends who repaired the torn or damaged parachutes, and their injured men, and brought the guys beer. Thankfully, much has changed.)

Most of the men were in the military reserves or worked at one of the nearby factories manufacturing weapons and fighter jets. Some had been to Vietnam. All in all, they were a genuinely congenial group, but I was quite a bit younger, viewed as an outsider and a hanger-on.

While some of the older men wanted admirers, I just wanted to jump out of an airplane, and maybe on some subconscious level to be a hero. To win acceptance, I bought beer illegally in Pacific Beach and shared it with my new heroes. Even so, in general, they remained diffident toward me. I was a college kid, and college kids were protesting the war. But unlike my female classmate and most of the others who came and went, I kept coming back. And fear was never part of the equation.

Early on, most of the training took place just by hanging around, watching, and listening. Then, at my third training session, we were allowed to participate in packing a parachute, but not to pack our own chutes. Even when they did allow me to pack mine, it was under watchful eyes—every time except on my seventeenth jump. Parachute packing is a very precise process with a lot of attention to sorting out and keeping straight the shroud lines (they connect the chute's canopy to a diver's backpack), to neatly folding the panels, and to exactingly placing everything in the backpack. The all-important D-ring for opening the chute is carefully placed in the pouch on the left shoulder.

Weekly training went on for a month before I was allowed

to take my first jump, with a long safety strap connected to my D-ring. Standing on a Cessna's wing strut looking down at the Earth and the target area was a deep gulp moment. The jump master shouted jump and I did. The safety strap pulled my D-ring and my parachute opened. My impression was akin to floating in water and kicking like a swimmer. The jump master commented on my kicking feet but signed my jump log and OK'd my next jump without the safety strap.

My second jump was the real thing. My trainee parachute had been packed for me and I went up with two others. I jumped! This time I had to reach for and pull the D-ring myself. But it had come out of its pocket and was flopping around over my left shoulder. So instead of a smooth cross-chest movement, face down, I had to turn my body to reach my shoulder to grab it. This unusual movement instantaneously rotated me from falling face down to a sideways posture with my right shoulder down.

When I grabbed the ring and pulled hard, the chute opened. I pulled on the control lines and got myself directed to the landing zone, turning around into the wind the last fifty feet. Perfect! As to my D-ring mishap, a quick inspection of the pocket that holds it secure revealed a loose thread sticking out of the seam. The chute had been used a lot by other trainees and was in need of repair. While there was no discussion about appropriate emergency behavior, that should have been a warning experience. Without the presence of mind to struggle to get to the D-ring, I could have been killed. To me at that time, it was just a technical problem. A loose thread!

The jump master, who had watched from above, laughingly acted out for the others how I'd been groping and kicking and falling sideways like the town clown. No problem. With this jump, I had been accepted as part of the pack by these older daredevils. I was in. It felt good.

❏ ❐ ❏

Even experienced jumpers occasionally puked in the plane, maybe from motion sickness. Afterward, they would joke about queasy stomachs or complain about not enough time after lunch or too much beer the night before. But, in fact, it was obvious that facing fear was a real issue for most. I suspect some had PTSD from the Korean War or were semi-suicidal for any number of crazy reasons. There were faces drained of color in every group I went up with.

Mostly we were quiet going up. The open door on these old prop planes made any talk short of shouting impossible. The engines were roaring as we gained altitude. One of our old jump planes had to be started by a man pulling down on the propeller. (In contrast to the bright and shiny perfectly maintained planes I had seen at Lindberg Field, ours were typically beat-up-looking six-passenger Cessna and Piper Cubs with chipped paint, small dents, and no door.)

A specialty of the jump master was to double-check that both plane wheels were chocked to prevent the plane from lurching ahead after the engine had fired up. He would pull down as hard as he could, then jump back when the prop was spinning so fast that it was literally invisible.

My cousin, Eric Anderson, who served as a corpsman in Vietnam, took up skydiving when he got back and was killed a few years later. It was a night jump, from a propeller plane. After pulling the prop to start the plane, he walked into the spinning propeller in the dark. This was a get-it-right, no-second-chance sport for sure.

A broken leg, a torn rotator cuff, or a broken collar bone from a bad landing seemed to be a rite of passage. They were so nonchalant, even proud of their injuries. On any given weekend I saw men in casts, and on a man who had broken ribs and fractured his spine, my first full body cast. He was still walking and pulled up his shirt to show off his cast. I wonder now if I subconsciously felt a need to have a serious injury to be just like my heroes.

Their making fun of my tendency to kick only encouraged me. As we waited for our turn to get a flight lift up, they would joke about bad jumps. To gales of laughter, mine included, one guy recounted how he'd been hanging from a telephone line; another was dragged across a field and ended up covered in cow poop. Disfiguring scars from smashing into a barbed wire fence or getting bounced along by a gust of wind and knocked into a pile of brush made for light-hearted banter, as did a story about how hard it is to cover your nuts with your hands as you realize you have missed the landing target and are going to straddle a fence. I did not laugh at that one. Fence straddling or missing the jump zone and getting caught on a telephone line was definitely not on my "must do" list.

But some things you learn the hard way. On one landing, I did not get turned into the wind soon enough and was pulled over backward on the ground by my fully open parachute in a fifteen mph wind. I felt like a skateboarder being pulled along the street by a pickup truck. Thankfully, I had a football helmet on for protection, a yellow helmet with the colors of my high school. What a joke for protection! But that is what the others wore, and I kept it for decades after my last jump.

Were they suicidal? Was I? All I knew was that I made new, tough-guy friends who had gradually accepted me. I asked questions, listened to their stories, brought them beer, and kept coming back.

When I was told to buy my own parachute, the only ones available were US Army cargo chutes that had been used a few times and sold off to war surplus stores after they got ripped or smashed. The Korean War was over and such stores were relatively common. I found one in the East County in a dusty shed of a building and went through a pile of opened cargo parachutes in a back row. There was not much room to spread them out to make sure they were not torn and that the shroud lines were in good shape. Finally, I selected the least beat-up chute I could find. It cost twenty-five dollars. For another dollar I got a duffel bag to carry it all. Striding out of that old war surplus shack was one proud, too big for his britches not-quite-adult, head held high, standing tall, proud as big red rooster idiot.

The following weekend I gave my precious purchase to a middle-aged woman who did parachute modifications for the club. She cut out two panels and added some lines with small black bulbs as handles to allow me to slightly close one of the parachute openings and thus steer the parachute toward the drop zone. She sewed up a perfect D-ring pocket.

For there on, every jump was a full body rush of adrenaline. I had gotten better, and without shouting about it to the old guys, was having the time of my life. Steering the parachute toward the landing target was easy enough, and I learned how to turn into the wind to slow forward progress before landing, even trying some free-fall maneuvers, including steering toward the group to hold hands, and some flips.

The plane ride up to elevation could be a teeth-clenching, hyperventilating experience. But usually, I would be focused and relaxed by the time I was crouched and ready to jump out the open door. There was no going back down with the plane. I had paid my money. I was on the wing strut of the little Cessna and the jump master had dropped the wind marker and positioned us. When he shouted "Jump!" over the engine noise, it was the moment of truth—and smirking, smiling, laughing, I absolutely loved the view and the rush.

Every night I was dreaming about what I would do on the next jump. To call it thrilling would be an understatement. These jumps were the all-encompassing activation of a whole-body primal alertness required to survive. To see the whole horizon coming up at you! Every nerve in your body firing double-time! What seemed like minutes compressed into seconds! I hungered for that feeling and wanted more. Without a doubt, I was addicted to the thrills.

❏ ❐ ❑

My seventeenth and final jump was almost my final moment in this body. Among the series of small missteps along the way, the first was with my boots. The trainer had emphasized the need to have high-tops to protect my ankles, so I got a pair of hand-me-downs from Dad; they fit my feet and went midway up to my calf. Good support, but with hooks so you could tie them up fast. Just a kind of two-handed back and forth to slip the boot strings over the hooks and you were ready to hike or jump. As it turns out, none of the other divers had boots with hooks. Theirs had strings fed through lacing holes. Why didn't anyone say something to me about the hooks?

The next issue was how I packed my chute. Since my fifth jump I had been packing it without much supervision. I could do it fairly quickly to give other jumpers access to the packing tables. On the day of the seventeenth jump, I had made one earlier, but when the pilot said he had enough fuel to go up again and the jump master asked for enough volunteers to pay the bill, I dashed to collect parking coins out of the ashtray of my wheels—"The Big Green"—a late-1950s Suburban van, another hand-me-down.

As the jumpers not going back up headed to the landing zone for a picnic, the clock was ticking until takeoff for me. But I still had to repack my chute from my earlier jump. There were only two long packing tables and my turn had not come up yet. The jump master said hurry up. Having packed my own chute at least ten times, I had it down pretty well. First, I got my rumpled parachute stretched out and folded the panels as I had been taught, and folded the shroud lines and stuffed them into the bag. Next, I did all the other steps but did them fast and maybe a bit sloppy in my haste.

In record time I was taking my seat behind the jump master, ready to roll for my seventeenth jump. It was to be at 4,600 feet, along with three others. I was the last one out, making an exuberant backward exit and hitting the tail of the plane with my left foot. Not a problem but it did give me a bit of spin. I spread my arms and legs and leveled out, getting oriented both to where the other jumpers were and to the landing site off in the distance. I had done this sixteen times before, so why worry?

Then I decided to make a delta position dive with my head down and feet up to get the rush of maximum speed, terminal velocity 175 feet per second. After a few seconds I glanced at my altimeter only to realize I was already at 2,000-feet and needed to pull my parachute ring immediately. I had passed the other jumpers on the way down. They had their own issues, but all three of them witnessed my rapidly unfolding drama.

With my head down and my feet straight up, I pulled the D-ring, which made the parachute open straight up past my extended legs. A bad decision, because the shroud lines crossed over my boots. Then the hooks on my hand-me-down high-tops caught some of the shroud lines. The parachute did not open. I was falling like a rocket, kicking hard and twisting like a fish hooked on a line.

Then the shroud lines came free! Some of the line shot up over the top of the parachute and friction burned holes in the top of the parachute. I looked up and saw sky through two huge holes in my mangled parachute. It was a lopsided Mae West malfunction! With holes where the nipples would have been. The right lobe was smaller than the left, causing me to spin in a circle. This should have been a moment of panic. Instead, I was pissed off.

I looked down, felt a rush of air, and instantly pulled the handle on the reserve. It popped out. Yahhhh. But it did not open. Boooo! I recall looking at it like it was a large white sausage hanging out in front of me. Then it was gone and I was still falling. Because I was in a slow spin, it wrapped around my body and according to one of the other divers watching me from above, made me look like a big white cocoon. In the moment, though, I was not afraid.

Maybe it was partially because I had been free-falling and play-falling, jumping and flying through the air since my childhood, when Dad constructed a huge swing set from lumber scavenged from the base where he worked. That swing set undoubtedly was a prelude to high school gymnastics and my training at the YMCA. Gymnastics also satisfied my urge to fly. But my gymnastics training, including flying rings, had, as it turns out, further prepared me for skydiving and thinking while in motion. As did surfing (essentially a controlled fall), water ski ramp jumping, and cliff diving in La Jolla.

Regardless, panic did not set in when the reserve chute failed to open. Rather, I swore and got to work, grabbing the white bellows of my reserve, pulling it around my body and pushing it out in front of me as quickly and hard as I could. The reserve chute opened in front of me, while the main chute—still as a Mae West—remained open. All the air resistance of the opened reserve chute pulled me toward it and my feet swung over a low brush. Together they slowed my descent enough to make it a survivable crash landing.

Just before landing my mind was screaming "Hit and roll." Roll to dissipate the force of the impact. It was only during this last half-second that fear overtook me, because the ground was right there and I knew I was moving fast! That instant is absolutely clear in my mind to this very day.

Hitting the ground feet first, I was knocked unconscious and do not remember much. No conversation with God or anything like that. Just out cold for however long it took a dozen men and women to run a quarter mile. When I opened my eyes and saw blue sky and a circle of heads peering down at me, they knew I was alive.

Somebody pronounced me "one lucky sucker" and with a little help I got my parachute in my arms and started limping, my legs, hips, and back sending rockets of pain up my spine with every step. I rode back to the airport in the back of a green pickup truck and sat on the tailgate hurting and quiet, listening to club members' versions of my presumed demise and subsequent resurrection. A good Samaritan handed me a beer.

After the men made a few jokes and one of them pantomimed my kicking and unwrapping actions as seen from above, the small talk moved on to other topics. Now I was one of them, for real. A wounded survivor. Conversation shifted to who was coming in next week to paint the training stands. No one volunteered to drive me to a hospital. It was a normal accident. Don't be a whiner. See you next week.

Eventually I got my kit and slowly put it in The Big Green, a solid-steel monster with a stick shift that taught me a lot about car repair. Though not really a go-out-on-a-date ride, it was perfect for the beach or shuttling neighborhood kids to school and lugging around jump gear. But on this day, driving a stick was a chore. Since I couldn't use my right foot, my left one had to handle both the gas pedal and brake. Awkward and clumsy, in the extreme. I stopped at a phone booth and called home, saying I'd had an accident. My dad, Frank, met me at the doctor's office. The doctor thought I had only a broken leg; the swelling was bad. The rest of me seemed OK. He suggested I get crutches and come back in a few days for a plaster cast.

At the doctor's, Dad and I chatted casually. With his hands gently probing my swollen leg, we had a WASP father-son moment:

Me: "I don't think I will do skydiving anymore."

Dad: "That is a good decision."

That's it. He did look away and up and I'm pretty sure he was thinking, "Thank God," although as an atheist he would never say something like that out loud. Mom never said much about the accident either. Her attitude was along the lines of: "He's a boy, what do you expect?"

With my cast and crutches, people would ask questions, but I would just turn around and hobble away. Finally, Mom said I should write it down and get over it. I complained, but finally got out the old Underwood. I was sweating. Drops started falling off my forehead. Periodically my hands would lock up. I froze for minutes, then start typing away. That account may be somewhere in a file on Easy-Rase paper. Here it is again, sixty years on, keystroked into a computer—but not as a brush with death that scared me straight. Instead, as I look back, it clearly set my course on what was to become a pattern.

I still note Mae West deaths in the news. They seem to happen often. Not long ago, a famous influencer died from a Mae West malfunction exactly like my own. Why did I live and so many others did not?

3.
BOUNDARIES & BORDERS

"I'm not a smuggler, I'm a missionary.
I have chosen to be obedient and not turn away from
danger. So when government says, No!, I say, Wait
a minute, God said, Go!, so I don't listen to the No!"
— ANDREW VAN DER BIJL

Dad **smuggled goods** across the US–
Mexico border all the time, but it was never thought of as
a big deal. According to family rumors, he had smuggled liquor
from Canada to Seattle while at college during the Great Depression, He was broke, had access to a small boat, and needed money. Perfectly understandable. And apparently, it became a habit.

Mom and Dad would take us across the border from San Diego in a small gray house trailer that had a kitchen, bathroom, and table with benches; it easily slept four, but my younger brother Greg and I preferred to sleep outside on green canvas army war surplus cots or spread out in the open in our sleeping bags.

Once, when we got back home and cleaned out the housetrailer, I discovered some lobster, rum bottles, and firecrackers secreted in the cleaned-up trailer's toilet bowl. I associated this casual illegal activity with the absolute joy of family camping and fishing trips. The excitement of the firecrackers and happy people, the catching of big fish, and the singing—it all coalesced in my young mind as good easy fun, and rewarding. We never talked about it, and I never thought through what might happen if Dad were caught. What I learned was boundaries can be ignored. Do your thing. Be discreet. Just don't get caught.

San Diego was the supply depot for the Western Fleet and sailors got shore leave when ships docked there. Both sailors and "jarheads" (Marines) crossed the border looking for booze and girls. Dad got in on the action in his own minor way.

By the time I started college, friends and I would go to Tijuana, a thirty-minute drive, sometimes every weekend. In the 1960s, Tijuana was a small, funky border town that essentially served as a recreation base for the Navy. The roads were bad and the buildings shoddy; little stores catering to tourists sold wide-brimmed Pancho Villa hats, leather belts, and Mexican toys.

Wild weekend party expeditions to Tijuana and fishing trips brightened up my early college days. We did crazy things like interview tourists for a sociology project, bet at the greyhound racing track, and frequent the Long Bar, where we could drink underage. We'd get drunk at strip joints, and sometimes thing got rowdy. Once I tried to see an older woman having sex with a donkey on a darkened, roped-off stage. And yes, we had awkward experiences with sex workers. It was weekend college life on steroids in a foreign country.

Things took a more serious turn when my cousin Larry decided to run away with his pretty and much younger high school girlfriend. He asked me to drive them to Tijuana on the sly. From there they planned to take a bus to Guadalajara. As I was crossing the border almost every weekend, taking them with me was not a problem. I dropped them off in Tijuana near a bus station. As I drove away, Larry was sitting on the curb of a busy street playing his guitar while his girlfriend nervously sat beside him.

I stopped for some street tacos and then drove back to San Diego without it dawning on me that I had helped an underage girl run away with an older guy to a foreign country. In my mind, I simply was helping out my cousin.

Predictably, panic spread among the families. The girl's parents contacted my Aunt Mary, Larry's mother, who called my mom, who interrogated me. I held out for a few days, but when informed the police were being brought in, I spilled the beans. About this time the girl and Larry came back home and everything settled down. No bad consequences for trafficking an underage girl. I caught a break.

A year later, heavier issues came into play. McCarthyism was sweeping the country. The local Kiwanis Club provided a scholarship to the university, and I was picked to attend a weekend anti-communist conference where wall maps showed the spread of this dangerous ideology, which supposedly had the US completely surrounded. Lecturers screamed about the "Red Menace" and demanded that we root out people with "un-American" tendencies. Afterward, I checked *The Communist Manifesto* out from the university library, hiding it under my shirt. The hysteria around the subject ignited my curiosity and further propelled my disdain for conventional boundaries. Communism as an idea was crossing borders all over the globe, and boundaries and borders were powerless to stop ideas. The hysterics of fat demagogues was something I wanted no part of. My ideas of right and wrong and good and bad were my own.

At the conference I met "Denise," who was involved with the Pacific Beach drug community—heavy stuff. We ended up dating, and witnessing together a talented left-handed guitar player go brain dead after sniffing glue from a dirty rag in a Campbell's soup tin half full of Duco Cement. After a few months, dates with Denise became too drug-focused for me. But drugs themselves were intriguing and I could not resist. Our romance was over, but she and I stayed in contact, occasionally smoking pot and cleaning out refrigerators in giddy frenzies of the munchies.

One day, Denise asked me to drive her and a girlfriend across the border. She was brash and demanding. Thinking I might finally get laid, I agreed. They were secretive at first, then Denise finally revealed that her friend needed an abortion. She had an address on the main drag of downtown Tijuana. We were to drop her off at a corner at a certain time, where she would be met and taken to the house where they carried out the procedure. I noted that the corner was near where I had recently spent time at what teenage boys then called a "cat house." The high-minded set called them brothels.

Denise's friend came out in less than an hour and I drove them back to Pacific Beach. I told my brother Greg but no one else. Denise never did let me "go all the way," but she did hook me up with a woman who was a bit older and agreed to meet me at a rundown motel. Maybe sort of an informal reward for services rendered. As my date smoked a cigarette and I picked at a torn edge of wallpaper, she asked if I collected scraps from no-tell-motels as mementos.

A few months later, Greg tracked me down at the university biology lab where I was dissecting preserved cats and asked me to take a girl he knew down to the same location in Tijuana. This was a huge surprise. Greg was going to college in San Francisco and said he hardly knew the girl but that she was an acquaintance of his girlfriend. Could I take them to the abortionist? I contacted Denise, who agreed to come along. A few hours later we were at the by now familiar corner in downtown Tijuana. Denise went off with the girl while Greg and I drank beer.

That we were, again, doing something completely illegal was not really part of our discussion. We were helping out someone in need. When the girl came back, I dropped her off at the San Diego Airport. I soon learned that she started bleeding badly on the plane and had to go directly to the hospital. That was the first time I ever considered serious trouble could result from transporting underage girls into Mexico to commit an illegal act. But the sexually compliant older woman Denise had introduced me to, along with a new job at the airport, combined to let such concerns drift into nothingness. Years later, when two different sexual partners notified me they were pregnant and having abortions without consulting me, I considered it to be Karma.

Even so, driving young women across an international border and in the process breaking stupid laws felt justified to me—and still does.

❏ ❐ ❏

The comparative ways money is handled was not hard for me to grasp, based on my numerous family trips to Mexico. When I arrived in Lagos in 1966, I carried notes and changed them at the bank. Then someone told me about the black market; the banks saw little of me after that.

Years later, in Burma (now Myanmar), my black market currency-changing came to a head. Our project manager encouraged us to bring as much cash as possible. Soon after arriving, my then-wife Cynthia and I were introduced to Ken, a local wearing a blue and white *longee* and button-down shirt. He asked if we had any money we wanted to exchange. We sure did! We had currency in a money belt and Cynthia's bra, and gave Ken a few hundred dollars. The next day his ethnically Shan, drop-dead gorgeous wife showed up with a paper bag filled with Burmese money. At the bank, the exchange rate was something like six Kyat to the dollar. Ken had gotten us seventy-to-one!

This became a pattern during my time in Burma, where the government simply could not manage finances. Corruption was so rampant that branches of the military competed for smuggling routes and natural resources. You never knew when the currency in your wallet would become valueless. As I traveled back and forth to the US, I carried various items into Burma for our research projects, including some outright bribes. The head of customs wanted golf clubs, so I brought him a nice used set. We were whisked through customs, despite some notable finger pointing and head nodding. Five minutes after we got to the rest house, the custom agent, still in his white uniform, showed up to collect his set of clubs.

□ ◻ □

Once, during my time in West Africa, my longtime girlfriend Patti and I were crossing from Togo into Dahomey at the same time refugees from the northern state of Nigeria were streaming south. Struggling during the post-colonial period, these small countries were ill-equipped to provide services for refugees, let alone a modern functioning banking system. As soon as we got through customs, we were forced to change money at the taxi yard, where we were overwhelmed by men shouting out exchange rates for our Nigerian Pounds. We picked a tall man who offered a better quote than the others and he led us over to a shelter at the edge of the yard. He asked to see our money, so I brought it out and showed him what I estimated we needed for a few days. He took my money and produced a rolled-up wad and started peeling off bills. His fingers were catching some bills in a way that let him count the same bill twice. Watching his hand movements made me real nervous.

Over and over, I shouted to Patti and whoever else was around, "Watch his hands." When he tried to hand us a wad of money, I refused to take it. I was not even sure if the bills he was counting off were the currency of Dahomey (now called Benin), or legal currency of any country at all. In Yoruba, which I had learned in the Peace Corps, I shouted, "Thief, thief." He gave us our money back and walked back to the small circle of other money changers, laughing. My reflex capacity to use words had come through.

The hotel staff subsequently told me the man I had called a thief was in fact a known troublemaker with a reputation for violence. In a land with little or no law enforcement, "Big Men" rule, as the Nigerians say.

❑ ❐ ❑

Then there was Pablo, a lively foreign exchange student from Chile I met at the University of Washington in grad school. He was Patti's office-mate in the Food Science Department. After he returned home, Patti and I applied for teaching positions in Chile at the *Universidad Catholica* in Valparaiso. We both got jobs, teaching salmon culture (me) and food science (her). Pablo told us to bring in some US hundred-dollar bills, and to change them with him, not the bank. The results, he assured me, would be fantastic. On the flight to Chile, Patti was a bit more voluptuous than normal, taking the risk for both of us.

A day after we arrived in Viña del Mar, Pablo came by and the three of us drank Pisco sours and ate *bistec a lo pobre*. He asked if we had the money and Patti produced the extra cash she'd carried in her bra. He returned with his jacket pockets full of Chilean currency, exchanged at many times the official rate. It added up to the equivalent of Pablo's annual teaching salary, and although we tried, we could not convince him to accept any recompense for his substantial risk. The authorities were handing out serious jail time for this type of activity. Later I realized we should have funded Pablo's Christmas party or made a generous donation at his niece's wedding. But our level of sophistication about cultural differences was not yet sufficiently developed. We thoroughly enjoyed Chile, even down to our awkward experiences with street thieves.

❏ ◰ ❏

Smuggling antiquities was a natural progression. My friend David and I recovered some ancient artifacts from Lake Atitlán, Guatemala. Somehow, I convinced my companion to dress as if she were pregnant, and she managed to carry a large, ancient clay pot with a jaguar head under her blouse on the flight back to the US. I refer to that pot, which I still have, as a relic of my "Indiana Jones" years. We were young! We did whatever we wanted to. The system was screwed. Screw the system. That was then. I have recently initiated the process of returning the jaguar clay pot to Guatemala where it belongs.

❏ ◰ ❏

The larger epistemological, economic, and environmental issues of smuggling fascinate me. We humans exchange things. Stuff for different stuff. Opportunities for other kinds of opportunities. We move stuff around. That is what we do. The process has been refined over the last few hundred thousand years. Moving goods (seashells), products (cloth, tools, weapons), or people (young lovers or girls who need abortions) across a territorial boundary controlled by another community without contributing to the benefit of the territory's leaders/owners definitely constitutes a breach of its economic rules. Moving then becomes smuggling.

Ecologically speaking, smuggling is like being a kind of

parasite. On an economic and ecological level, it merges our exchange culture with that of the natural biological system (parasites, symbioses, and hosts). A smuggler is akin to a parasite that lives off the host but does not benefit the host. Symbionts, on the other hand, contribute to the well-being of the host by declaring the goods and paying to move them across borders. Being a scofflaw and breaking community standards is a different situation entirely, of course, having nothing to do with biological relationships.

❑ ◻ ❑

How did I get away with smuggling and money laundering activities? For one thing, I was always a small-time player, just below the radar. Also, I was comfortable about deceit. Sneaking around the system was fun, in and of itself. It fed my appetite for risk. Now, I absolutely consider myself an honest man, but during my youth, boundary crossing behavior was something between "What's the big deal?" and the adrenaline rush from an intoxicating macho experience, something to brag about over beer and pizza.

As well, I have come to believe that my largely innate, semi-instinctual ability to read people and situations is due to my upbringing. My nurturing, risk-taking parents exposed me to different kinds of people and languages. Finally, paying wary attention to enforcers comes natural to a kid who got his butt smacked with a razor strap when he was completely out of line. Not often, but it happened. Those were different times—there was still corporal punishment at schools!

This mix of early experience—including learning music, earning Boy Scout badges, camping, hunting, gymnastics, and fixing things that are broken—gave me skills and abilities that both emboldened me in risky situations and helped me survive some serious scrapes. (Music, in particular, may seem odd to mention in relation to risk. But hear me out: playing music is good for the brain. It is both a situational attunement facilitator and a full brain operation/control factor. Functional Magnetic Resonance Imaging (fMRI) shows that brain hyper-activation occurs when playing with others, which requires being in the moment and blocking out extraneous noise and other factors. This may be a stretch for some but I am pretty sure I am right.)

Being "smart" does not exactly equate with some of what I did, but being situationally smart enabled me to get away with it.

4.
REDNECKS WITH AXE HANDLES

"Our lives begin to end the day we become silent about things that matter."
— DR. MARTIN LUTHER KING JR.

At a gas station in Montgomery, Alabama, a group of white shirt-and-tie locals loitering under some shade trees advanced, seemingly to block my access to the bathroom. Three of them carried brand new axe handles, Paul Bunyan-style, a kind of a rude impression of knights fingering their swords. The wood was almost white. There were no metal axe heads on the handles, which had obviously never been used to cut down trees or split logs for a fire. As I pushed my way into the men's room and locked the door, I could hear them talking softly and moving around outside. If they attack me, I told myself, they must know they'll be arrested. There was a highway patrol car across the street; two GI's with rifles stood on the corner. Then I thought again. Fat chance! Southern justice at the time was anything but impartial. The signaling system in the center of my being became a honking, screaming siren.

At St. Louis University (SLU), I had been taking Taekwondo, but I was barely accomplished enough to get out of a one-on-one confrontation without a bloody nose. A small mob with weapons called for a different approach. So I adopted the stance emphasized by our hard-nosed ex-Marine instructor, who repeatedly stressed the need to get out of a fight as more important than winning it. "Keep your emotions in check," he counseled, "and walk away whenever possible." With that in mind, to the extent that I had any strategy at all, it was to ignore the axe handle thugs. Not to be frightened or engage them either with unnecessary words or physically. Just do a Jesus thing and slide through their angry ranks.

Slowly pulling the bathroom door open, I saw the broad backs of several white shirts. These were big guys. I paused and quietly said "Excuse me," sliding between them using my left shoulder, stepping out slowly, casually, and not once looking back.

Had I been traveling by myself, instead of with two women, and had it been later in the evening, the outcome could have been far different. Maybe the police car across the street deterred them? Just as likely, the officer was their friend. My own friends, Liz and Eulanda, had witnessed the encounter and were as shaken as I was. We were in the Deep South to march with Dr. Martin Luther King in Montgomery, a national focal point in the push for desegregation. Northerners were unwanted; local rednecks considered us all outsiders and revolutionaries.

The initiator of our pilgrimage was Elizabeth, a new friend who went by Liz. She had waved her arm and shouted in my direction, so a lot of people around could hear, "Hey Bob, do you want to go to Montgomery and march with Dr. King?" My answer was an immediate yes. What Liz did at that moment is true leadership: knowing intuitively what needs to be done and doing it, while trying to engage with others. Who knows, maybe she wanted a guy to along so it wouldn't be just women in her small group, but I am pretty sure if she hadn't enlisted a man, she would have gone anyway. She was committed.

We were in the graduate program at SLU. Liz was a real scientist, studying entomology under the guidance of Dr. Fear—yes, that was her name!—whereas I was still adrift, a pretender and a good enough student, if just barely enough. But the classwork was demanding, and there was no way out of hunkering down to study, memorize, and write actual papers.

So to decompress, I indulged in distractions that shielded me from the horror in the news all around me. I take little pride in confessing that at the time my first priority was to stay out of Vietnam, and to play music with new African American friends and meet freshmen girls. Ya, drink beer and eat pizza.

It is true that I'd had the occasional thought about joining the Civil Rights volunteers, but it is also true that until Liz challenged me, I could not get off the starting block. Beyond hanging out with the cleaning staff and going to East St. Louis to see the talent, resourcefulness, tenacity, and self-respect of the men and women of color around me, I was all good intentions and no follow-through.

Meanwhile, my master's project on imprinting singing patterns of other species of birds on newly hatched song sparrows took me out to the countryside to identify nests and set up recording equipment. It was fun and easy. I loved it. My major professor, an animal behavior expert, was a smart, dedicated Jesuit and a motorcycle-riding physical fitness addict.

The City of St. Louis, Missouri, and the University itself had been rude awakenings for this San Diego surfer kid. In my time at the prestigious Jesuit institution, I never saw a person of color who was actually a student. This on a campus directly across the street from a shanty town that practically advertised institutionally supported poverty.

My exposure to overt racism was mostly based on living in an almost all-Black neighborhood, where I went to lively block parties and on weekends hung out with Black musicians and frequented a few pretty funky taverns in East St. Louis. I heard blues and jazz, and was exposed to a lot of eye-opening, soul-grinding poverty. I saw a white, uniformed police officer reach out to fondle a young Black woman at an ice cream store; and witnessed white policemen chasing a young Black man, laughing as they swung their clubs at him when he hid beneath a car; and walked past numerous "white only" and "colored" bathrooms on weekend trips to the countryside for spelunking in limestone caves. And I had been called a "nigger lover" by a drunken voice in a crowd for talking to a Black friend, who was sadly unsurprised and told me to "just ignore him, that happens all the time."

Policy stances at SLU were by no means forward-thinking either. Beyond its lack of Black students, there was its staunch support of Catholic Doctrine on abortion and divorce, its tacit support of segregation, its wretched history of child sex abuse. None of this sat well with me or suggested they would approve of attendance at a voter registration rally in connection with Dr. King.

Nonetheless, I had to play by their rules, as much as I could stand it. Though I had little interest in Catholicism, SLU had been the first graduate school to accept me and seemed a suitable place to avoid being drawn into the horrifically stupid Vietnam War. I was there tuition-free, with a small stipend as a teaching assistant, and free from the draft, for now. (This came after a full ride as an undergrad at a Methodist college—another sect that did not interest me, but which also gave me a deferment.)

❑　❐　❑

We were now three, after Liz recruited Eulanda to join us in our journey to the Deep South, which we saw as taking us into

America's heart of darkness and evil. Eulanda was from Panama and nearly as tall as I was, with a Mediterranean complexion and a winning smile. She was weeks shy of finishing her master's degree program and had accepted a job with the CDC in Atlanta. She expressed surprised that more students from the university were not going. Along with her brother, she had been in demonstrations and riots in Panama since they were "old enough to carry a flag."

I had no romantic involvement with either of them. That part of my life was focused on Pia, a charming freshman from Denmark who shared my interest in spelunking; we learned to rappel down cliffs into caves together. We rappelled with a team into limestone caves to collect bats. We used miner-style carbide headlamps and slid through narrow bat-guano-lined channels in long undulating caves. We practiced killing our lamps and then relighting them in the dark with muddy hands. No way to find our way back in the absolute darkness. Which was truly scary. We held hands.

After Pia passed on our invitation, and since my vehicle, the earlier-mentioned Big Green, was truly on its last leg, we decided to take Liz's old yellow VW bug and drive practically non-stop in order to get to Alabama and back in time for Monday classes. But first, there was the matter of our responsibilities as teaching assistants. Skipping our Friday shifts for a long weekend required approval by the dean of the School of Biology, who on my first day at the Biology Department had told me to cut off my short beard. I doubt if any individual hair was more than an inch long. Hell, I was a California beach kid and considered shaving optional. Even so, I went along to get along and cleaned up for the jerk. After which, disgruntled but clean-shaven, I deliberately slow-walked past his office a few times.

The immediate supervisor of the biology teaching assistants

was Father LaFleur, a Franciscan monk who was supportive of our going. So we begged and bribed others to cover our classes. Then we had to meet with my nemesis, the dean of the Department of Biology. Liz explained that we had recruited substitutes and would only miss one class. He heard her out, looked at the three of us, then abruptly turned around in his chair and reached for a special phone on a bookshelf behind his desk. He then barked at the operator to connect him with the provost, the top Jesuit at the university. When the provost came on the line, the dean delivered what he thought was his death blow: "I have these three graduate students that want to join the demonstrations down South. I want them expelled. Immediately!"

We were in shock.

Expulsion would have been a disaster, especially for Eulanda. She was an immigrant whose family members were now all in the US. Her job offer with the CDC would probably have been withdrawn and she might even be deported. And I would lose my student deferment and find myself slogging through rice paddies, getting shot at by men and women passionately defending their country.

Ignoring us, the dean listened to the provost, before putting put down the phone, clearly unhappy with what had transpired. With clenched fists planted firmly on his desk, he slumped forward and in a guttural snarl demanded that we "get out of my office, now." He didn't have to tell us twice!

Shaken but with renewed resolve, we made preparations. We knew that what we were doing was radical and dangerous; it was impossible not to. We had all read numerous news stories about idealistic students who suffered injuries, serious beatings, and even fatalities by doing just what we intended to do: stand up and be counted. But we knew we had to go anyway. Before we left, Father LaFleur slipped me a few bills for gas money, whispering, "Please do not tell anyone."

Looking back, I believe that through this trip I was unconsciously remanifesting the commitment and ultimate sacrifice of many relatives mentioned on family occasions. In particular, a faded daguerreotype above the family piano stood out for me. It depicted a relative holding a battle sword with a rigid arm, fused at the elbow lost fighting for the North in a Civil War battle.

Then there was my great-great-grandfather, George, who was on his way to Washington, D.C. to report for duty with the Union when the train derailed, crashing into a freight train taking on water. He was one of fourteen survivors out of fifty, and due to his slow recovery did not directly participate in any major battles. He spent his recovery years in the home of a prominent Quaker family headed by Robert Gibsen Jones; the family was likely active in the Underground Railroad that helped enslaved people flee and find refuge in the North and Canada. I like to think that George helped the Quaker family protect and shepherd men and women fleeing slavery, which would have made him a people smuggler like me.

❏ ❐ ❏

Daily, we had read in the reputable *St. Louis Dispatch* of the atrocity of segregation and government policies that enshrined it. Men, women, and children supporting the right to vote and to drink at the same fountains as white people were being sprayed with fire hoses, and worse, sometimes murdered by sworn officers of the law. Clearly, something was seriously wrong south of the Mason-Dixon line, and we were showing up to be counted.

We did not talk about this much in the car. We had started out in the early evening, planning to drive all night. St. Louis is only about six hundred miles from Montgomery, but the roads were terrible and there were rumors of speed traps.

All three of us knew that the South was home to people who saw us as invaders. In their hidebound minds they were fighting back. I saw all Southerners as inbred and hypocritical, which was no doubt a generalization, unfair to many good people. They were probably a mix of truly bad people and others who just would not stop something unjust from happening, no matter how demonstrably wrong.

But we were on a mission, and our attitude was that of Admiral Farragut, who in a Civil War battle at sea ordered his men: "Damn the torpedoes! Full speed ahead!"

We arrived in Montgomery early the following morning, and followed signs to the rally point. We finally parked the VW in a Black family's backyard near the St. Jude church, about three miles from the capitol building. Then we hoofed it a considerable way to the rally, which was easy to find, thanks to newly built elevated wooden platform for speakers and performers.

When Martin Luther King spoke, his powerful voice carried like a protective cloak of the angels of truth, moving the throng with the felt intensity of the moment. Our dedication and collective commitment united us. All three of us were engulfed by body-shaking streams of tears. To have heard his distinctive tones in person is one of the peak experiences of my life. We had come far and were exhausted, but his speech energized us, galvanizing our commitment.

After that, Peter, Paul and Mary sang a few songs and we started marching and singing "We Shall Overcome." We walked for hours. Initially, we marched six abreast down the center of the street. As the morning went on, we dropped arms and sang, as only highly motivated people can sing, not afraid to die for what they believed in. Racism was evil, and more evil as governmental policy. It had to be struck down. We identified with the early Christians who sang in the Roman Colosseum as they were attacked and devoured by lions. To call Dr. King's words inspirational is an understatement.

I remember more tears as I sang along: "*Deep in my heart, I do believe, we shall overcome someday.*" Roars of anger coursed through the multitude. The whole crowd started doing a visceral, James Brown style "ruff, ruff" that scared me a little. It was war-like. We were at war.

I have no doubt that white racists felt temporarily outnumbered and afraid just then. The marchers, conversely, were energized. To a person, we were willing to walk into the jaws of death, be beaten and hosed and attacked by dogs. King set the bar really, really high. We listened and learned and were prepared to reach that high standard of secular ethics. Racial discrimination may be common, but in that crowded street we were making a statement: segregation was evil.

On some of the side streets there were rows of armed soldiers. They stood "at ease." Their rifle butts were at their sides, and one arm behind their backs. It seemed that two uniformed military officers would follow any local police. As we marched, we asked African Americans on the sidewalks to join us. When I reached out my hand to one man, he withdrew and brushed me away. We did not stop to consider that it was even more dangerous for them than it was for us. Many of the horrific details only came clear years later. At that time, we were pretty ignorant of the depth and lethal magnitude of the problem.

Toward the end of the march, a young Black woman stepped down off the sidewalk and took my hand. We walked and sang together for a few blocks. Then she broke away. She was brave, the future of the South that we wanted to support.

After the march, we did not have any thought of looking for a place to sleep. The armed men on the side streets and the tension of the crowd put us on alert. We were in "get out of Dodge" mode. On the outskirts of Montgomery we stopped for gas. That's when the rednecks with axe handles did their best to menace me. But my need to relieve myself was urgent and I was not about to soil myself because of some bullies with "outside agitator" issues, while the highway patrolman and the two GI's looked the other way. We made it back in St. Louis fourteen hours later.

❏ ❐ ❏

I see myself as a pussycat, nonconfrontational up to a point, a sort of passive-aggressive personality with poor boundary management. But there are times when I have felt compelled to take a stand. Marching with Dr. Martin Luther King in Montgomery both echoed actions by my ancestors and erected the foundation on which my later support of social justice was built. And we got away with it! Liz's leadership was a key factor, along with my martial arts training, in de-escalating confrontation that undoubtedly saved me from injury or even death.

In retrospect, it feels like a peace-loving Quaker's spirit manifested to use my body in its timeless quest for justice and a peaceful resolution of conflicts. I am proud and happy to have shared this seminal experience with Liz and Eulanda. We did a good thing that day.

Baby Bud with father and grandfather

Playing the French horn while sister Susanna sings and brother Greg plays the violin

Music was a big deal—and so was my Pachuco look hair in the 10th grade

My mother Mildred, a nurse, who adopted and fostered children in need, and was a very good businesswoman

My father Frank, a U.S. Navy scientist with 40 patents

*Fearless warriors in imaginary canoes
ready to fight pirates*

*Swinging bar, trailer home for camping trips,
little sister on the run for the swing*

CHEST CHUTE NUMBER	TYPE JUMP	ALT. JUMP	DELAY SEC.	MANEUVERS	DIST. TO TARGET	SUR. WIND	REMARKS
AN 65	DF	3	5	stable	100+	5	ok
an 65	DF	3300	5	stable	70	5-8	
an 65	DF	3800	8	STABLE	60	5-8	good
AN 65	DF	3800	10	STABLE	110	5-8	
AN 65	DF	4400	10	STABLE (almost)	130	7-12	
65	DF	4600	15	Right turn	14	45	
65	DF	4600	15	turns R+L	out	5-7	*#@!! ———— may west, broken ankle

*Record of my last jump in a war surplus cargo parachute —
resulting in a broken leg and crushed ego*

Examining the jaguar head clay pot, Guatemala, 1972

Deer hunting in the Cascade Mountains with a 12-gauge shotgun

Captain Bud with blue marlin and deckhand Steven, kneeling

As Captain Bud, the party animal

Back to science on the Mini OTEC
(Ocean Temperature Energy Conversion)

*Marriage ceremony between Bud and Cynthia
in Kailua-Kona, Hawaii*

A family at last

Surveying a site for the new marine science center
in the Sultanate of Oman

Ugbongway village, with Warren, my dugout canoe buddy
in the white shirt, Nigeria

5.
THE EPHEMERAL AWARENESS OF DEATH:

Adventures with the Peace Corps in Nigeria

"Those who make peaceful revolution impossible will make violent revolution inevitable."
— PRESIDENT JOHN F. KENNEDY

When our plane touched down in Lagos, the first thing we saw were tanks in the streets and soldiers behind sandbags around government buildings. We soon learned that officials, senior military leaders, and the Sultan of Sokoto had been killed during a coup d'état. In 1966, coups were considered normal in Africa. The legacies of colonialism were being overthrown, and a Nigerian coup was seen as a typical Third World event that would not affect us. Soon, though, an atmosphere of menace surrounded locals and Peace Corps Volunteers (PCVs) alike, in the build-up to the Nigerian Civil War. Eighteen months later, I would leave the country at gunpoint.

After abandoning my master's program at SLU in disgust, I'd chosen the Peace Corps as the best option to retain my draft deferment; and I was over the moon when the assignment to Nigeria came through. Africa! One of my earliest memories was crawling around on a big, blueish, foldout *National Geographic* map. Dr. Albert Schweitzer was a hero of my mother's. Also, the ubiquitous greeting "Dr. Livingston, I presume" had made the continent a locus of childhood adventure fantasies. Classic comic books like *King Solomon's Mines* were catnip to me.

The three-month PCV training took place on the side of a hill, something like a farm camp, outside Frederiksted, St. Croix, in the Virgin Islands. We lived in tents and we ate in a rustic mess hall, studying Nigerian languages five hours a day. I was placed in the Yoruba language group. To say the least, Yoruba was challenging, with its five tones—three level tones and two contour tones—not to mention implosive sounds totally unfamiliar to English speakers. But it was one of the main languages of Nigeria and learning it to some degree was required to stay in the program. I absolutely did not want killing or injuring someone in Vietnam on my conscience, so I studied hard. (Through the grapevine, I heard that one guy who'd been booted out of the program was drafted the same week.) The setting was tough going, but I was fully committed and in my element.

Others did not find the training so congenial. In fact, about a third of our group left the program before completion. Some were pulled out due to psychological issues. Scary stories told by returning volunteers may have contributed to some of the hurried exits. Other trainees went home simply because they could not adjust to the rustic conditions in the campground and the muddy trails between tents. Being on a farm and jungle hillside at the end of a dirt road was certainly distinct from the brownstones covered with ivy they were used to. The defections from our ranks continued through our arrival in Lago: one PCV initially refused to get off the plane.

During this preparation period, we were interviewed both by staff and visiting psychologists. I remember being called into the side tent three times. One trainee was sent home after telling the staff he was going to marry a local waitress in Frederiksted.

There was also gossip that the camp director's wife was doing too many quality-control inspections of one particular volunteer. It seemed that she needed to check out his sailing technique in a small, rented sailboat with a covered cabin. She wore a small yellow bikini and bent very low in front of the trainee as she entered the cabin. We were all young and rushing with hormones, and the story spread like wildfire. Then the volunteer disappeared. Indiscretion with the boss's wife was a sign of poor judgment. Off with his head. Go to war, kiddo! You win the Virgin Islands PCV Training Program Darwin Award.

The camp director's spouse was indeed cute, but I had my eye on Patti, a good looking fellow recruit. At training camp, she and I began a seven-year love affair. Patti was there for many of my subsequent escapades in Africa and Latin America. I thought of her as a kind of wing woman, but she had her own appetite for risk, independent of me. I really think she targeted me, and I could not say no to this terrific woman.

We had a wonderful few years. We made love in the jungle, on tramp steamers, and next to a stream where chum salmon were spawning. She was beautiful, smart, and daring; ours was a fantastic pan-global love affair that on one memorable evening in Canada saw us drinking rum punch and dancing until the tiles came off the floor.

Toward the end of the training, I was sent to the small volcanic island of Montserrat, in the Leeward Island chain of the Eastern Caribbean. The entire population, other than a few Canadian snowbirds, were descendants of African slaves brought to the islands to work on British-owned plantations.[1]

I was placed in the home of a local teacher and spent my days studying Yoruba and wandering around a small village on the

[1] Sadly, in 1990 the Montserrat volcano erupted, forcing the evacuation of the whole island. The Canadian snowbirds that owned houses there lost everything.

southern side of the island. Montserrat also exposed me to disaster, death in the community, and a near fatal accident. As well, I encountered costumed stilt walkers, bullwhip crackers, and hawkers with big aluminum trays of food on their heads. They were much like characters I would later come across in Nigeria.

These were truly visceral, get-ready-for-Africa experiences, among them torrential rains, a flash flood on the tail of a hurricane that killed two milk cows grazing in a rocky, brush-filled ravine. The cows drowned, having been tethered to stakes driven into the hard ground. Since there was no refrigeration available, they were set to be butchered immediately before the heat and moisture spoiled the meat. I showed my Swiss Army knife, all three inches of it, to the owner, who instructed me to cut away the skin from the muscles. On exposed volcanic rock, I sweated and worked with the small knife until I had blisters.

During that time I befriended Peter, a tall, lean local with a small rowboat who took me out fishing and collecting conch. The Queen conch is among the biggest marine snails in the world and can weigh up to a couple of pounds, counting its thick, massive shells. It has a poisonous stinger used to kill other marine snails such as cowries and turban snails. Peter slowly rowed and I used his makeshift glass water-box to look for giant conchs on the sandy bottom. I had small fins and a good face mask, and when I spotted one he would stop the boat directly overhead. Then I would carefully lower myself over the side, dive down, and bring them up.

At least that is how I did it after the second boat exit. On that ill-conceived occasion, I backflipped off the rail and the tiny dinghy completely capsized, dunking Peter. The two conchs I snagged on my first dive immediately sank to the bottom. Peter was very diplomatic, informing me in his deep-throated Caribbean Pidgin English, "Don't do like that, man!" Hanging onto the boat from opposite sides, we laughed, and righted the dinghy, and bailed it out using our hands and my dive mask to flip water out.

Then I dove to recover the two conchs that had formerly been in the bottom of the dinghy. The shallow ones were easy pickings, fifteen to thirty feet deep. As we worked our way into deeper water, I was soon free diving fifty feet deep or more. After several hours of swimming and diving, I was getting tired, and we already had almost a dozen conchs. This was to be my last dive of the day.

My ears cleared easily as I went down, but the view through the mask was slightly altered due to the angle of the dive, and as I got near the bottom the conchs did not seem to get closer. There was also a distinct current. Then, when I reached the first conch, grabbing the big shell in my right hand and swinging around to get the second one, I had my first throat spasm. I grabbed the other conch, but dropped it almost immediately. I'd been looking up at the bottom of the boat and wasn't paying attention to my hands.

Circling back to get the dropped conch nearly killed me. My throat seized up, time squished to eternity, and my vision went to checkers as I broke the surface. I hung off the side rail of the skiff for a long few minutes gasping for breath, realizing I had nearly blacked out underwater. (I later learned that shallow-water-black-out is fatal unless someone can bring you to the surface.) But, the episode passed and I shook it off. That Sunday afternoon, Peter and I had conch stew with descendants of the very people I was going to be living with in Nigeria.

WELCOME TO NIGERIA

In Lagos we were greeted by the Peace Corps Mission staff and each given a box of books, a first aid kit, and money for a bicycle. I was shuffled around for a couple of weeks, then ended up sharing a neat teachers' house at a private school for the country's elite, where I met Warren. He had been there for almost a year and seemed to feel he was not doing much for poor Africans or seeing Nigeria at all. He spent virtually all his time in the large private school compound behind high walls and chain link fences.

Eventually, I was assigned to the Federal Government College at Warri, Midwest State, to teach in a Higher School, sort of the equivalent of an American junior college. The taxi trip from Lagos to Warri took me into the heart of the Niger Delta. It was an arduous ten hour journey. The roads were bad and the drivers were exhausted, stoned kamikazes, playing chicken with oncoming taxis, seeing who would blink first. Often, we were behind a long line of enormous overloaded lorries and European cars that had to slowly navigate deeply rutted mud paths beside collapsed sections of a washed-out road.

That day I ate my first "bush meat," which included the un-appetizing and troubling sight of a monkey hand floating on the surface of a big iron cauldron of stew at a roadside kitchen.

Warri was an oil boom town in south central Nigeria where Shell and other multinationals were exploring, drilling, and shipping oil to Europe. People from all over Nigeria and West Africa came to Warri to find work. We PCVs had not yet linked the coup and onset of the civil war to oil extraction and the lop-sided distribution of revenues from exporting it. This was of less concern to us than the million details of safe travel, school, and living supplies—and getting on with our assignments.

About a week later, I was at the main taxi yard in Warri with Tony Nwabaku, a gracious local and a teacher at a primary school who had taken me under his wing. He quickly became a friend and invaluable resource, teaching me drumming rhythm patterns, guiding me into forest villages, and instructing me on what I should not do relative to student sensibilities and culture.

He also demonstrated how to forcefully deal with a local man who was harassing a female PCV.

Tony also introduced me to the Warri Expatriate Club, the local watering hole for expat oilmen. The club was essentially "whites only" and consisted of a drinking pub with tennis courts. Within its confines, I grew accustomed to hearing the drawls of Texas and Oklahoma oilmen bemoaning how Nigeria was the armpit of the world, but the money was great.

On this day, in the taxi yard, Tony casually gestured at a trash-littered site. From his off-handed manner, he could have been pointing out a public market for fishmongers, but he wasn't. It marked the location of a recent "human sacrifice." I paid little attention to the phrase human sacrifice but it planted a seed. Intertribal conflicts and the specter of human sacrifice lingered in the background of local news and my mind almost every day during my tenure as a PCV.

Growing Up Fast

Danger and the swirl of death constantly surrounded us all, local and PCV alike, even though I was essentially emotionally untouched by the ephemeral nature of tragedies woven into the cacophony of daily life. In fact, I never cried for any of the dead I knew during my time as a PCV, not until much, much later.

Horrific sights were all too common. I still remember how helpless I felt watching a young man get severely beaten for stealing an orange in the local market. He was doing a snatch-and-run when the sellers, buyers, and onlookers converged on him and exploded into action. The beating and kicking were ferocious. I did not linger to find out his fate. Those two-hundred-pound-plus Nigerian market women were strong and tough. They had to be! They could carry a hundred pounds of yams and fruit on their heads for miles, and wield heavy wood mallets to pound yams for hours. A kick to the head by one of these women could certainly kill a man.

Two of my own serious scrapes involved Dr. Taylor, the PC doctor for the Mid-Western Region of Nigeria. One afternoon the two of us were on a balcony of the PC office building in Benin and saw a dusty commotion on the street below. Sorting through the maze of moving bodies, I slowly realized that the melee centered on our office car and its driver. He was trapped on all sides by shouting people with waving arms, who formed an angry mob as they beat him. Dr. Taylor and I hurried downstairs and approached the scene. Popular among the PCVs and administration, the driver was from a different tribe than the Benin City locals. His shirt was torn, hanging off his shoulders, and his face was swollen. A fresh dent and some paint scrapes on the front left fender suggested that he had been in a minor traffic accident.

As we rather cautiously approached the crowd around the driver and car, a young man grabbed Dr. Taylor's wallet out of his back pocket and started to run. Reflexively, I grabbed the pickpocket's free arm and swung him around in a big circle, knocking him against other people, and with two quick steps slammed him noisily up against the PC car, forcefully threading my arms under his armpits, my hands pushing down on the back of his neck to place him in a full Nelson, with his belly against the car door and my knee in the middle of his back. He had been quickly and successfully immobilized by a very amazed PCV, me.

The pickpocket had dropped the wallet when I was swinging him around. I looked over my shoulder and saw that Dr. Taylor had recovered it and the driver being beaten had slipped away. The mob scene de-escalated, and I heard some people say *oyibo*, local slang for a white man. I let go of the pickpocket and we briskly walked back to the PC building, prudently keeping watch over our shoulders.

In hindsight, I could not believe what I had done. To this day, I still can hardly comprehend it. I was not, and am not, a street fighter. Despite taking Taekwondo at university, I had never been even close to engaging in a physical fight back when schoolyard fistfights were routine in middle school. Frankly, I was afraid of the guys that got into fights. I was a musician, and one of the skinniest, sickliest kids in school. I had rheumatic fever in primary school and middle school, and numerous bouts of upper respiratory infections, causing me to miss years of school. What I did have was a family inheritance, the ability to talk my way out of almost anything with a few apologetic words, a smile, and shift in body language. And after all, I was in the Peace Corps in the first place because killing and fighting seemed very strange to me.

I don't remember the driver's name, but eventually we became friends and drank Star Beer together and laughed about the incident. I guess I should remember his name, because some months later he saved my life after I got sick while giving a biology lecture to my second-year students. Sudden chills came on fast, mid-sentence, causing me to stutter as I lectured. Abruptly, I dismissed the class and peddled my bicycle back to my nearby quarters in Ugbongway Village. Shivering, I crawled into bed. Then, with superhuman effort, I put on every article of clothes I owned and covered up with a few sheets and thin blankets to assume the fetal position and try to sleep. Next, I got feverish and started vomiting. Too weak to keep running to the bathroom, I had the cook bring me a pan to set beside the bed. I did not eat anything for days. I could barely hold down water.

Medical staff required all PCVs in Nigeria to take a pill once a week to prevent malaria, the number one killer disease worldwide. We typically took our pill on Sunday. Already during my stay, I had had worms, hepatitis-A, and various GI tract problems, so I took my "Sunday Sunday" chloroquine phosphate tablets religiously. Now I was sick again, no big deal. My village friends checked in on me, mostly saying simply *oyibo doo*, which translates roughly into "I feel sorry for you, white man." *Doo*, a compassionate expression for anyone suffering, carried a sort of fatalistic recognition that bad stuff happens. But no one did anything.

I think it was on Friday when I got sick; someone at the school should have checked up on me but no one did, though even in my debilitated state, I should have dragged my sorry ass out of bed and gone for help. Instead, I just lay there sweating, shivering, and vomiting out of my mind with fever.

After about four days, the driver we had seen being beaten by the crowd showed up and literally lifted me out of bed, wrapped my arm around his shoulder, and walked me, dragging my feet, out to the car and drove me the two hours to Benin City. I was delirious, laughing a lot and hallucinating bright, kaleidoscopic colors on cattle horns and tree vines as we drove. Trees, cattle, and roadside plants were surreal in my giddy state. The driver rounded up Dr. Taylor and they took me to the local hospital, where the staff tried to get some pills down my throat, which was anything but easy, since nothing had stayed down for days. Finally, Dr. Taylor told me sternly to keep the pills down unless I wanted to die. I remember retching but holding the vomit in my mouth and then re-swallowing. After the hospital, Dr. Taylor left me at Patti's house in Benin City to recover for several weeks before returning to Warri to continue teaching.

After that I don't remember seeing the driver again. I think he went back to his tribal village in the Eastern State. But thanks to him, a stupid PCV who couldn't admit he had malaria is here to tell this tale instead of rotting in the ground in Warri, a modern victim of what in Kipling's day was referred to by colonials as "the white man's grave."

IBADAN

About six months into my service, Dr. Taylor found a cyst on my left testicle during a regular checkup. He recommended that I immediately go to the hospital in Ibadan and have it removed because he couldn't be sure it wasn't cancerous. In Ibadan, I stayed at the Peace Corps guest house, built on a hill, with a deeply rutted red dirt road as the only access. It was just across a wide ravine from a federal government military garrison. On the evening before the operation, I missed the scheduled dinner at the guest house, so made my way to the corner food stall at the foot of the hill intending to buy a beer and a snack. Just as I arrived, the stall's owner was briskly shuttering the doors. He refused to sell me anything. As I pleaded with him, a convoy of heavy military vehicles came slowly rumbling down the road. Some were filled by soldiers with rifles.

When I asked the owner what was going on, he answered simply, "Soldier business." Later in the evening the shooting started across the ravine at the garrison. Gunshots and explosions went on for several hours, and then the sounds of women screaming started. We poked our heads out of the building carefully, to watch the explosions and try to figure out what was going on. The next morning, we found out the trucks were full of Northern soldiers who had come hundreds of miles south to attack the garrison, where lead officers involved in the coup were staying with their families.

The early morning cook and staff said soldiers had killed all the Igbo soldiers and raped the women, cutting open the bellies of the pregnant women and smashing their unborn children against the walls. This kind of savagery was shocking, but the PC guest house staff spoke about it matter-of-factly.

Even with all this going on, my cyst had to be attended to, so without breakfast I got a taxi and was soon in the hospital's operating room. An American-trained Nigerian doctor told me that they did not have adequate anesthesia, but they were going ahead with the operation regardless.

Four NFL-linebacker-sized Nigerian men appeared, one pressing down on each of my shoulders, the other two holding down each leg. I was given a tongue depressor wrapped in a washcloth to bite down on. I bit hard when I felt the scalpel slice into my left testicle, and tears filled my eyes when it felt like the surgeon was scraping the tissue. I remember trying to talk but only rasping, telling the surgeon I couldn't stand much more of the pain. He pressed ahead, then showed me a brownish gray ball the size of a small marble. Then, without ceremony, I was walked over to a narrow, hard wooden platform in an empty room. No mattress. No pillow. No warm blankets. Nobody around. I was in excruciating pain, and thirsty. When I repeatedly called for assistance, no one came. After about a half an hour I started having violent stomach cramps, such that I could not sit up or shout for help.

Eventually, I managed to roll off the platform onto the floor, crawling on my hands and knees out into the hallway, calling out as loud and often as I could, which was not loud at all given my cramps. When I reached an interconnecting corridor, a woman in street clothes led me, stumbling, out of the hospital to a spot on the road at the side of the hospital. She flagged down a taxi, which took me to the road leading up to the PC guest house. I groaned when the driver of the aging taxi said he could not make it up the steep, slippery, deeply rutted driveway.

It was extremely painful to walk; my testicles had swollen up to the size of small grapefruit. It was step, gasp, pause, step. At the guest house I collapsed into my bunk bed. The next day I learned that Northern solders had gone to the very hospital where I'd been, to finish off some escaped wounded soldiers who were Igbo. The Northern Hausa soldiers went room to room, killing Igbo patients, doctors, nurses, and technicians.

I recovered and went back to my teaching job in Warri. Months later I learned the soldiers had not killed my surgeon or the lab technician and that my cyst had been benign. What a relief. The pain was gone but memories of the screams of the tortured and dying families linger to this day.

THE OLU OF WARRI

In one of our walks early on, Tony Nwabaku took me past the jail, where inmates rhythmically chanted as they cut grass in the prison compound with long thin machete blades. Their cadence and humor fascinated me, as did seeing inmates with knives. They were looking at me and singing, chanting, and laughing between chanted tonal phrases. It was clear that their humor was at my expense. Their refrain contained rhymes with *oyibo* (roughly, a peeled-skin person), which were echoed by an ever-changing mob of small children following us shouting "*oyibo, oyibo, oyibo,* give me pin" in Nigerian Pidgin, which Tony translated as akin to "White man, give me a writing pen."

When he thought I was ready, Tony said I must meet the "Olu of Warri" or Big King of the town. The Olu is a designation given by the federal government, based on practices instituted by the indirect-rule philosophy of the British colonial service. We arrived on foot at the two-story house of the Olu and were met by a thin man who told us that to meet the king we would have to go in on our knees, spread our arms, and loudly proclaim "*Ogy ami shawoo, Ogy ami shawoo, Ogy ami shawoo.*" We had to say it out loud three times while tilting back our heads to expose our throats. The thin man demonstrated the salutation and we practiced, then followed him upstairs and were ushered into a room where we did exactly as we had been shown, our knees on the concrete floor as we loudly shouted the greeting three times. (Those words, which were unintelligible to me, were to take on significant. life-saving layers of meaning a year later.)

The Olu was a big, heavy man seated in a large brown wooden chair. He had a colorful wrap of cloth on his head and a dark red and yellow wrapper around his waist. Two massive, bare-chested men on either side of his capacious armchair had machetes in their brown leather belts and metal tip spears. Their faces were cold, unsmiling.

I briefly told them that I was to be a teacher. Tony explained my status in a mix of Nigerian Pidgin and one of the local languages I did not know. It might have been Urhobo or Igbo. The only words I could make out were "Peace Corps," "teacher," and "America." There was more discussion and a nodding of heads; all in all, things were going well. Then the Olu produced some local gin called *kai-kai*, in a rectangular bottle that resembled a quart of Johnny Walker. He splashed some on the floor out of customary respect for his ancestors. The liquid was clear as water. The Olu offered me a small metal cup that he explained as "Push me, I push you." I drank in sips before foolishly draining the cup, thinking that would shorten the duration of my torture on my knees. It was fiery strong, like drinking straight shots of gin. I grimaced. They laughed.

After fifteen minutes, we were instructed to rise. Slightly stooping, we faced the Olu and backed out of the room. As we left, I noticed a large wooden desk stacked with a pile of papers in colorful A-4 type folders—and what appeared to be a human skull repurposed as a pencil holder!

A HOUSE AND A CANOE

When I started teaching, the Federal Government College was still under construction, and a cranky Welsh engineer supervised a team of locals. His Nigerian foreman was imposing and friendly, taking me under his arm and showing me around. The Welshman shouted at the crew making the cinder blocks from crushed stone and bags of cement. He told us he had to stay on top of the workers every minute, since they would try to steal handfuls of cement to sell in town. When they did that, the concrete blocks would fall apart and he would have to start over.

He pointed out the one completed house on the site and said I could move in whenever I wanted to. The two-bedroom, one-story structure had reddish corrugated iron roofing and was situated up against the lush green mangrove jungle at the back. Out a window there was a small winding channel in the mangrove. Immediately, I imagined a dugout canoe, all mine, parked behind my house to use as I pleased.

At the market near the Warri River there were dozens of tied-up dugout canoes with a bustle of activity around them, largely consisting of loading and unloading goods such as fish, fruit, goats, and baskets with unrecognizable contents. Having grown up between Ocean Beach, San Diego Bay, Mission Bay, and Baja California, I had fished, surfed, and water skied from all manner of boats, so I asked Tony about buying one. His responses were evasive, but I persisted.

After moving into my house, which was a ways from town, I was treated like a guest by the Nigerian foreman. Together, we spent the late afternoons talking about local culture and walking to adjacent bush villages. He taught me how to carefully follow game and people trails, while stepping around animal traps and staying vigilant because of snakes, including deadly, spitting cobras, pit vipers, and black mambas.

In these small crude pop-up villages of bush huts we would sit on rough-hewn wooden planks eating from a metal plate slathered with cooked cassava and bush meat, and washing it down with Star Beer. These economic immigrants from other parts of the country were happy to meet the *oyibo*, and I began to pick up snatches of Nigerian Pidgin in their huts where we all found much to laugh at together. The foreman, for his part, talked about ritual murder involving local communities and secret societies as if it was normal.

Finally, the English headmaster arrived, and a few weeks later, Warren, whom I had met in the capital, did too. His school term had ended, and to him Warri was like the Wild West compared to Lagos. Tall and thin and very organized, Warren moved into a new white concrete block house next to mine. He was a dedicated math teacher, as evidenced by his evening activity of solving calculus problems for fun while I was reading and preparing my biology and chemistry classes.

During this time, my mission to secure a dugout canoe paid off, with the help of Tony and a village elder named Orastus Okoromadu. We traveled downriver, where on a remote island riverbank Ijaw craftsman built boats and canoes. A short ways into the dense mash of mangroves and brush, the trail opened up into an area of the forest cut and cleared by Ijaw craftsman to create a boatyard with huts on stilts. Soft gray smoke from dozens of small fires, along with the shadows of people along the edge of the clearing, made the scene look like something out of a Bruegel painting. The aftereffects of a morning rain left droplets of water in the air; combined with the smoke, they turned the lush vegetation into a misty aura, at first foggy then dark and impenetrable.

For larger diesel-powered crafts, the boat-building process essentially entailed felling a tree and shaping the trunk into a keel by burning, chipping, and contouring the outer shape, leaving a hollow center. Towering trees over a hundred years old, with massive, spreading buttress root systems, made for valuable boat wood.

As we made our way toward the center of the clearing, the workers briskly slipped into the dense forest, as if our presence had created a bow wave. Further, the government endeavored to control logging operations and this improvised boatyard was undoubtedly illegal.

One thin, nervous, middle-aged man, bare-chested and wearing only a blue and gray wrapper around his waist pulled up to mid-calf, met us warily near the center of the clearing. A halting discussion in a mash of tongues ensued. Our boat captain was Ijaw but he also spoke Urhobo to Tony. Tony and Orastus spoke Nigerian Pidgin and English. Additionally, Orastus spoke Itsekiri while Tony spoke Urhobo. For my part, I gawked and pretended to listen. From the Yoruba I had studied, I could follow bits and pieces of the Itsekiri.

This boatyard produced watercraft much larger than the two-man canoe I wanted. We left in something of a hurry. No joyful come-and-eat greetings. No shared drinks and offering to the ancestors. We were strangers and it was appropriate to fear strangers. Human sacrifice was common and no one wanted to be the next ritual offering.

A month passed, then out of the blue Tony said my canoe was ready. We went to the quay at the public market where what I saw dismayed me and it showed. Brand new, the canoe was black from the fire-based construction process; it had no seats, only small-diameter branches wedged into the sides to keep the charred and wet wood from collapsing inward.

After some palavering, heads started to nod and there were smiles. Orastus, as the village elder, had a solution. I was told to pick up a used canoe at Ugbongway village, with the understanding that it was mine in the afternoons but that the village people could use it in the mornings. Tony and Orastus had come through, and the *oyibo* had his canoe.

Canoe trips soon became the highlight of my weekends. Along with Warren or Patti, I would paddle out into the winding mangrove branch channels of the mighty Niger River Delta. The Niger is huge, on the order of the Mississippi River, with nearly a million square miles of watershed flushing heavy tropical rains from the mountains of half a dozen countries. It winds over two thousand miles, finally entering the Atlantic Ocean in the vast Delta of large and small channels where we played with my canoe. During the rainy season, the water level may rise some twenty feet, covering adjacent land. During the dry season, the level falls dramatically, exposing formerly submerged islands.

Due to suspended sediment, the water in the mangrove channels was generally a dark brown. Thus, there would be little light penetration into the water. As the tide rolled out, exposing the sediment, the benthic algae would get abundant light and grow rapidly, producing a wealth of nutrients in the mangrove soil. During these low tides, small goby-like fish (mudskippers) would crawl out of the water, using their pectoral fins like short arms to pull themselves up the mudbanks. Completely out of the water, they would vigorously scrape the thin pellicle of algae off the surface of the mud with their broad big-lipped mouths. Seeing these fish crawling around on land made it easy to conceptualize the evolution of fish to walking land animals.

MONKEY CROSSING AND A GREEN SNAKE

Once we saw a band of easily over a hundred gray monkeys swinging from the top branches of the mangroves. We paused in our paddling and just watched the amazing, endless line of them crossing overhead. They chattered and walked hand and foot style, each following the monkey ahead of them, in a long line, tree to tree, over the same branches, over the river channel, looking down at us suspiciously.

Hanging from branches or swimming in the river, snakes were a common sight, but a large green snake trying to get into our canoe was a different matter. I was in the bow and Warren was paddling in the stern. I spotted the snake swimming ahead of us and then lost sight of it. The snake was halfway into the canoe before we knew it. Warren crouched and poked at it, as the canoe rocked perilously. We both nearly jumped into the water. Had we done so, I'm not sure how—or if—we would have gotten back to shore, since we were in a wide channel with thick, dense foliage on either side, dominated by red-rooted mangroves. No dry land in sight.

Rather foolishly, we had never practiced or even discussed what to do if the canoe capsized. We carried water and a small machete, but no life vests or signal flares. Much to our relief, the big green snake surrendered to Warren's stabbing and pushing harassment and slid back over the side. This type of green snake turned out to be nonpoisonous, but hindsight is always twenty-twenty.

A River Blessing

During the period that turned out to be the run-up to a horrific civil war, one event sticks with me. Warren and I encountered an old man and a child at a confluence of channels. They were fishing, and when they saw us, they paddled over and handed us a small aluminum coin. The man pointed at the child with a big toothless grin. He wanted a blessing for his grandson. We were clearly a novelty of note in that part of the Delta. Regardless, I was the one who felt blessed by that old man and child fishing for their dinner in a deep channel of a mighty river.

My lasting impression of those I met on canoe trips was of their friendliness and generosity. To some locals, the "White Man" was still special, worthy of a small donation for a smile and blessing, but to others we were devils manifest in their midst.

Teaching Nigerians about Nigerian Ecology
—and England

I loved teaching biology, and tried to weave in knowledge of the magnificent mangrove ecosystem around the edge of the college. My stories provided fun opportunities to connect my students to the rich ecology of their environment, where green and reddish brown snakes hung from the lower branches of trees in narrow channels, and their color pattern blended in with mangrove roots and overhanging branches, as small, pretty, blue-crested kingfishers darted from tree to tree, trying to catch unlucky mudskippers and other larval fish using the mangroves as critical habitat. A bird that mistook a snake for a mangrove branch became its lunch.

But mostly I focused on the Higher School Syllabus, to give my students the knowledge to graduate, which entailed passing a nationally mandated examination. That meant teaching them to learn the plants and animals of the UK in our British syllabus! Ridiculous but true.

For my own edification, I never tired of reading and studying the Niger Delta ecosystem of interwoven channels, and the ocean-liner-deep channels of the main river. At times I would wonder whether as PCVs we were the deep sedimentary channels or the water in the river. Were we pimps for a corrupt civilization or simply vehicles, like the kamikaze-style taxi drivers, participants in an overwhelmingly complex process beyond our comprehension?

The No-Snake Zone

Snakes were disturbingly ubiquitous, both around the grassy grounds of the college and my white brick house at night. When I prepared my lessons in the evening, with the lights on, the crash and snap of insects smashing against my windows, and the croaks of frogs and toads outside, were like the background din of a war zone that I grew to ignore. The frogs and toads were eating the falling insects. The smaller vipers were feasting on the toads and frogs, and the larger cobras and mambas were feeding on the toads and small snakes. I kept a long, stout stick by the door of my house. It was actually a branch of a tree with a forked end and all the bark peeled off. I named it the "Snake Stick" and in the evenings did not leave the house without it.

To supplement my Snake Stick, I relied on the groundskeepers who kept back the jungle and cut grass to keep them at bay. A small, muscular groundskeeper called Shorty would bring me dead black mambas, cobras, and rock pythons, which gave me the chance to show my students that a snake's fangs were the dangerous issue, not the tip of the tail. Shorty was a happy man but one day I was told he had been killed by local people. Students had seen his body on the side of the road near the college. He was Igbo. The Urhobos and Ijaws in that area hated the Igbo.

MOUSE ONE, SNAKE ZERO

Interacting with snakes was one of my hobbies in the first year. A teacher laughed as he told us how he shook out a small green snake hiding in the toes of his day shoes. Everyone had snake stories. It was like talking about a football game or recent movie. "How's the weather? Seen any snakes today?"

The school would not let me take snakes into the classroom. Both teachers and students emphatically told me that no matter what kind of cage or box, they would not come to the school if I had a live snake in the room. So when Shorty brought me a small rock python, about two feet long, I put it into a box-cage with a glass window that a local carpenter had made me. I kept it in my house on top of the bookcase, where I could watch the python through the glass front. Shorty also brought me a field mouse to feed the snake.

The next morning the little rock python was dead! I was shocked. The head of the snake had been chewed up and the mouse was sitting in the corner breathing hard but very much alive. Unbelievable? A mouse, about an inch-and half long, had killed a snake two feet long that outweighed it a hundred to one.

I asked Shorty for another rock python and mouse, and this time watched them intently. As the snake approached the mouse, and coiled for a strike, the mouse jumped over the snake's head, and with a flick of its own head, grazed the top of the snake's head with its teeth, landing to face the snake, crouched in the opposite corner of the box. The snake turned around and again slithered toward the mouse, coiling for a strike. The mouse jumped again, barely glancing its mouth on the top of the snake's head, which I could now see had small irregularities, like the scales were ruffed up. After the third attack, I knew the snake was going to be killed. I resolved to let both animals go.

When I did so, the snake rapidly avoided me and went to the floor and coiled up in the corner of the house. James, my cook, was wide-eyed in disbelief and fear. I reached down to grab the snake and it bit me on the thumb. I had the briefest moment of pause. Yes, I was absolutely sure it was not poisonous, and there was no bleeding, no shooting pain. But now I was pissed! After my nice glass box and trying to feed mice to it, my pet snake had had the poor manners to bite the hand that tried to feed it! So, using my left hand to slowly move toward the snake and distract it, I grabbed it just behind the head with my right hand. As the angry snake coiled its body around my arm, I carried it outside and tossed it in the tall brush between the house and the mangrove creek.

Of course, the snake had been right to bite me. It was an artificial situation and my experiment with the box-cage resulted in the death of one of its cousins. Looking at my thumb several times, I could feel the bit area and see the tiny punctures but nothing else. My lesson plan for the next day needed to be sorted out. Such was life: insects hit the window of my lit-up room; frogs croaked; snakes ate mice, other snakes, and frogs. I had learned, the hard way, to stay out of the way of natural processes. And that African mice were really, really tough customers!

COBRA FIGHT

About the same time, I had a fight with a cobra. Walking home after school, I spotted a sizable black snake darting across the front yard of my Scottish neighbors. The husband taught English and his petite wife had her hands full with two small children. They were a lovely family. I had seen this big black snake once before near Warren's house, but it was gone in a flash. Now, here it was again, stretched out so that I could take in its size, easily five feet long and several inches thick. The biggest snake I had seen since a massive tree snake slithered down the hallway of the school building toward my classroom.

I initially took this one to be a black mamba, an extremely dangerous, fast-moving, and very deadly poisonous species. Shorty had brought a dead mamba to the school once and with a pencil I'd pulled up the fangs for the students to look at. They stayed at least three feet away even though it was obviously dead.

This five-footer, however, was very much alive and in the front yard of a home where two small children lived. Something in me locked in to express my role as a protector. It needed to be dispatched immediately. As I got closer, it turned and darted into the small culvert under the driveway. (The entire college was set up with drainage channels, and every house had a driveway over a large PVC pipe to allow water to run off during torrential rains.)

Rushing home, I grabbed my trusty six-foot Snake Stick, the one with a fork at the end. Patti followed me with our household machete. Carefully crouching in the small drainage trench, I looked into the culvert pipe and saw the snake coiled up. When I jabbed it, the snake reacted by exiting from the other end of the pipe and shooting straight up the driveway toward the Scottish couple's house. In hot pursuit, I took an awkward whack with my Snake Stick and hit it mid-body. The snake then turned toward me and reared up, spreading its hood.

This was no mamba! It was a spitting cobra, a species with small holes in the front of its fangs, and was maybe six feet from me. Spitting cobras shoot their poison at the eyes of rats. Tony had told me that in traditional thatch roof homes, when rats fall from the ceiling, you know there is a spitting cobra in the house.

A bolt of realization struck me: this spitting cobra might shoot poison into my eyes! I instinctively turned my whole body away from it, seeing, in the waning late afternoon sunlight, droplets of venom in the air to my right, elbow high.

Turning my back to this extremely angry spitting cobra fighting for its life was not advisable. I swung around to face it. The cobra's hood still flared, as it closed the distance between us. Now it was less than three feet away. Wildly swinging my Snake Stick, I managed to catch it behind the head, then flip it a short distance away. As it straightened out and headed back toward the Scottish family's house, I hit it hard, from a both-arms-overhead wood-splitting-lumberjack posture, smashing downward and bashing the snake just behind the head. It writhed in a tight trembling coil. When it stopped moving, Patti handed me the machete and I cut the head off in one wild swing. It was an adrenaline-rushing few minutes. I tried to act calm but I was anything but!

By this time I had a full audience. Other teachers were there, and the Scottish family watched from their front steps. There were a few "har hars." My Nigerian neighbor even clapped. I amped it down to a sort of awe shucks feeling and picked up the warm body of the snake, feeling the inner musculature still moving. For some reason, I felt the need to skin the cobra instead of simply dumping its body in the trash. Snakes skin easily. I kept the skin without curing it. In a couple of months it started to fall apart and went into the trash anyway.

Though I did the right thing to protect the community, I still feel sorry for that spitting cobra, which, like the little rock python, was just doing its snake thing. To them we are an exogenous threat, to be fended off with spit in the eyes that can cause permanent blindness, or by biting, like the rock python had done. A big cobra bite could have proven fatal. NBD! Just another day in the Niger Delta.

EXPLORING THE DELTA BY CANOE

PCVs were constantly warned about the dangers of all manner of snakes, including big boa constrictors and fast-moving mambas, and of huge crocodiles, not to mention bandits, but Patti, Warren, and I were not concerned. We were giddy, happy to make another bicycle trip to the outlying villages and go for a paddle in my dugout canoe just for the fun of it on most weekends and holidays.

Warren and I did make some long canoe trips to unexplored channels and once bicycled to a remote village and spent the night. The small coins we gave to helpers, ferrymen, and guides along the way were, in turn, enthusiastically pushed into the hands of embarrassed young women with infants on their backs. The men would place a coin in the palm of the woman's hand and then fold her fingers back on the coin.

If she accepted the coin, the young men making the offer

would display a whole range of emotional excitement, from a sort of grateful hands-against-the-chest movement to a swaying shoulder-tipping dance with a huge smile. Money was rare in the heart of the Delta villages and our small contribution to the Delta economy made some people very happy. The vast wealth created by the country's oil never touched these abjectly poor but happy Nigerian villages.

6.
HARBINGERS OF IMPENDING DISASTER:
Exit without a Strategy

"Thank you for the tragedy. I need it for my art."
— KURT COBAIN

Maybe the first major message we received that Nigeria was not the place to be in such turbulent times was on a trip down a side channel new to Patti and me. It started when we saw some palm fronds woven into an impression of an arch. Although palm fronds were readily used in the market or at small roadside stores for shade or to make brooms and sleeping mats, we had never seen anything like this arch. It called to mind a walkway to a church on Palm Sunday. Two sturdy tree branches supported the woven fronds. The arch was clearly man-made, and judging by the still green color of the fronds had been maintained. Depressions in the muddy bank told us that canoes had recently pulled up right in front of this curious archway marking the entrance to a trail into the mangrove forest.

We cautiously made our way about fifty yards into the forest, where we came to a small clearing. There were machete marks on the brush and some tree branches had been chopped off. We walked head down out of a sense of caution; innately, when we got to an open clearing, we knew we were trespassing.

Small branches and leaves were scattered across the floor of the clearing; the open area was about ten yards wide. Off to the right we saw a crude, four-legged stand about three feet high. This was something completely out of place in the mangrove forest. Looked at closer, it seemed like a rudimentary jungle pulpit. It was held together without nails, only by twisted vines. At the base of the stand were some bones. Because of their curvature, I initially took them to be goat horns or rib bones. Short-legged goats were everywhere in villages. I loved Nigerian goat meat stew with *garri* (steamed, fermented cassava root). I often went to a restaurant near the taxi yard just for their *garri*.

Upon brushing away some leaves and twigs, we realized the curved bones were human ribs, of a dull gray color with small patches of greenish gray mold here and there. There was no soft tissue at all. The bones were not scattered as would have been the case had wild animals been feasting. The leg bones were directly where they should be related to the human hips. The arm bones were placed directly adjacent to the scapula and shoulder clavicle.

After we cleared away more leaves, it hit us like a thunderbolt: we were looking at two complete human skeletons side by side; but neither had a head! We looked around for skulls to no avail. It was a stand-up-straight "Oh my God" moment.

With a collective shudder, we backed away, at first slowly then trotting fast back to the canoe, praying that no one had seen us go up that trail. A few days later I recalled the skull I had seen on the Olu of Warri's desk. The whole business of human sacrifice was coming into focus. It seemed that not all sacrificial victims ended up at the taxi yard.

HEADY STUFF

The local newspaper occasionally had articles about bodies without heads. After a year in Nigeria, I was not surprised, shocked, or even dismayed by a piece about a human body found decapitated near the local football stadium. Normal stuff in a land pulsing toward war. During an evening drinking beer, a local teacher told me about another teacher, a local albino, who'd been taken away for human sacrifice. There was talk of secret societies that required a human sacrifice in order to join. Local tribes were constantly picking off someone from another tribe based on the belief that a member of that tribe had placed a curse on a person who died from it.

In addition, the paper and radio and gossip told of mass killings by northerners of southern tribesmen working up north. Almost any trip to town took me past the taxi yard and exposed me to truckloads of refugees from the north with bandages on their heads and arms. When they had recovered, revenge would be required. A vicious cycle.

Plus, it was not unusual for the bodies of oil contractors to be shipped home from accidents and malaria. Death was such a common fact that stories of violent ends simply washed over me like the evening news about tornados in Arkansas, hurricanes hitting Florida, or mass traffic accidents on a California freeway. But those things happened to others, not me! I had my work to do. A bubble of ethereal boundaries surrounded me. Until much later, I do not recall any emotional connection to these injured and dying people around me. Maybe a flash of compassion here and there, but in general I was oblivious to the crush of pain. Somehow, I had to stay focused on my job as a teacher to block out the cacophony of hurt and rage all around me.

PIRATES AND EMERGENCY WORDS

As we came around a tight bend, a long, high-sided canoe carrying four of the most terrible-looking men I had ever seen confronted us. They were ragged and fierce looking by any measure: one had a single eye, another wore a blue bandana. They all had large knives in their cloth belts. Spotting us, with a grin and a shout they plunged their paddles into the water and rammed our canoe, pushing us up on the tangle of mangrove roots at the riverbank. Things happened fast. In the front of my canoe, Warren faced the lead river pirate. Trying to stand up, he was rocking our canoe precariously, as I looked at the small machete in the bottom of the canoe.

To say the least, we were not expecting this. We were not far from the village, just down the mangrove channel, on our way to join up with the Warri River. Of all the things I could have done in this terrifying situation, I used words. I did not pick up the small machete, which would have been useless anyway against four big men with weapons. I did not scream for help or try to run away or cower in submission.

What I did was speak words, and not in anger or fear. In simpler terms, I reflexively attempted to talk my way out of an almost certain death. The specific words I spoke somehow came out of the depth of my soul, consisting of a phrase I had not used in over a year, since genuflecting before the Olu of Warri: "*Ogy ami shawoo.*" I shouted it emphatically, like an order to stop, spreading my arms wide, chin up, as I had been instructed on that occasion.

The pirates froze. It was like stop-action cinema. Nobody moved a muscle. I recall the second man in the pirate canoe bending forward, his hand slightly raised, locked into place. The pirate staring at Warren, so close to him they may have exchanged sweat, looked at me with piercing wide eyes. There was no movement at all in the back of the canoe where the leader was seated. They all just stared at me. I don't know why, but I shouted "*Ogy ami shawoo*" again. Then a third time, even louder.

The pirates came unfrozen at that point, sitting down in their canoe and paddling backwards, turning their canoes around with rapid strokes, leaving as fast as they could with the rhythmic guttural sounds of heavy muscular exertion. They did not do a walk-back "Yah-OK" to my incomprehensible (to me) performance. They ran away as fast as they could!

We were badly shaken and paddled back to the village double-time. We did not exchange a single word on the way. After discussions with locals and connecting dots in a life stream of experiences in Nigeria, I came to understood that through my verbal outburst of a phrase I had heard only once, a phrase which held no meaning for me, the river pirates knew we were under the protection of the Olu of Warri, the Big King. Maybe they were afraid they would be hunted down and the Olu or his minions would take their headless bodies to a clearing in the forest.

In the moment, what I did was totally unconscious, without forethought. I now believe that there is a module of the brain that stores "escape words" for when needed the most. This key word storage and retrieval process may have its roots in the evolution of language. Another attribute of the human brain to be studied. A genetic gift from the past. One that saved my foolish ass. Thank you ancestors! Thank you very, very much.

A Hausa Warrior

Among the striking characters I met in Warri, Suli stands out. He was a Hausa from the north, over six feet tall, with deep smallpox scars all over his face and bare shoulders. When I met him, he carried a small wooden bow a couple of feet long and a quiver of iron-tipped arrows. He wore a sword in his wide leather belt that had been pounded out of corrugated iron roofing. He then demonstrated some hand-to-hand fighting techniques. His gestures struck me as humorous. The muscles of his bare chest flexed and stood out below his skin. He was very thin.

Suli was proud and elegant in his poverty, and when he asked if I needed his services as a sort of personal security detail, I respectfully agreed to hire him. The timing was right, since small thefts were occurring while we were teaching. Suli got right to work, keeping an eye on my neighbors' houses and mine during the day. I never knew where he stayed at night. He came and went irregularly, and I never cleared his employment with the principal. One day, James, my cook, said he had seen Suli's body in the street. He'd been killed by locals, refugees from the northern cities who had lost everything in the pre-Civil War ethnic cleansings. He was from the wrong tribe in the wrong place in violent times.

Juju Killed Victor

Also etched in my memory are encounters with Americans in addition to the five PCVs teaching in Warri. On a trip to Benin City, I met Claudette, a pleasant, well-educated African American from North Carolina. She was a traveling school inspector for the Mid-Western Region, evaluating them for government subsidies to help upgrade the quality of education in the countryside. Before coming to Warri with her Nigerian husband, Musa, whom she'd met while he was attached to the UN Peacekeeping operation in the Democratic Republic of the Congo, Claudette had worked there, also for the UN. Musa became fascinated with her, walking over thirty miles round trip from the garrison to see her on weekends.

Tall, happy, charming, and upbeat, Musa now worked for the Benin City Police Department. They were a lively couple.

One evening in particular sticks with me, when Claudette, Musa, Patti and I dressed up in our best *agbadas*, sweating, drinking, and dancing to "high life" music in a big circle for hours. Patti and I were immersed in the dance of life; the beat of the music and intensity of the times led to brief trancelike moments of union. We were all in one endless line of humans moving to the vibration of drums, rattles, electric guitars, and eternal change. The morphing by evolutionary processes of ecosystems, cultures, and the human experience.

As part of her job, Claudette visited schools near Warri. Her government per diem was abysmally low and she was typically forced to stay in cheap local hotels that operated mostly as noisy, heavy-drinking brothels. So when she asked if it would be alright to stay with me, we worked out an arrangement whereby she could stay in my second bedroom when necessary. We developed an excellent, mutually supportive relationship from which I learned much about the challenges faced by small schools in the jungle.

The following account about Claudette's eventual fate is pieced together from several sources. It started when she became fed up with Musa staying out to all hours carousing with other women, and gave him an ultimatum: Come home late, drunk, smelling of other women one more time and "I'll leave you that same night." Meaning business, she had her suitcase packed.

Soon after, Musa staggered home drunk again with the pungent perfume of another woman all over him. The working women at local hotels and restaurants traditionally used heavy perfumes and scented waters. As good as her word, Claudette grabbed her bags and dashed to her car and started to drive away. Musa ran after her and jumped on the hood of the car, but when she killed the engine and abruptly stopped, he slipped off onto the ground. Moments passed. Then she started the car again but could not see him. She assumed he had gotten up and out of the way. Gunning the engine to drive away, she hit a big bump. Stopping the car, she saw that she'd run over Musa's head. He died instantly and Claudette was jailed. For the next weeks, publicity swirled in the newspapers and by word of mouth about the American who had killed a Nigerian policeman. Her trial was quick.

Claudette's salvation came in the form of a story circulating about a woman from another village who felt jilted by Musa and had gone to a famous and powerful witch doctor to place a lethal curse on him. Juju was every local person's dread. It was black magic. Truly lethal. That story proved enough for the judge. He ruled that the village woman and witch doctor were responsible for Musa's death, and poor Claudette was simply the innocent victim of a process started years ago by ultra-powerful forces beyond human control. She was set free and put on a plane the same day. I've always wondered whether the witch doctor story was concocted by lawyers to get the political awkwardness of an American woman in a Nigerian jail for the murder of her philandering Nigerian husband out of the papers. I would have loved to hear her version of events, but lost track of her in the confusion of the times.

NEVER KICK A ROOSTER

After about a year on the Government College campus, I moved to Ugbongway village, where I kept my canoe. It was a quick bike ride from the college to the village and they needed housing for the new incoming teachers and their families. I moved into a brick house owned by a Federal Government judge who lived in the capital. In time, I entered into village life. Every afternoon the headmen of the village sat on a massive log and small benches on the side of the street at the entrance to the village. It was sort of a men's club; mostly they discussed their farms and their problems with the women in the village. Lots of first, second, and third wife issues, and teenage boy problems.

On the way home from teaching, I would stop and chat with them, practicing my feeble Yoruba/Itsekiri much to their amusement. Around us, small, short-legged goats and chickens roamed freely; it was not uncommon to see them trawling for food scraps. One day I saw one of the elders kicking at a large rooster that was pecking at the ground near him. The rooster, however, did not take being kicked lying down. It leapt, flapping its wings and launching itself in the air straight at the man's leg, slashing him with its long, sharp, chicken-warfare spurs. The elder's ankle had a narrow slit; a trickle of blood slowly appeared. They all laughed; they were farmers and it was nothing more than a scratch. It sure looked like more than a scratch to me, but what did I know about the rigors of farming slash-and-burn plots of land in the jungle. They grew yams, cassava, peppers, and *ganja*. Some raised laying chickens. Everyone fished, owned a few laying hens and short-legged goats.

About a week later my cook said that the elder was very sick and I should go see him. He was lying rigidly on a woven palm frond mat on a wood plank bed, his arms tightly flexed near his chest, with the small of his back arched off the mat. He was in the final stage of a fatal tetanus infection, with a table knife wedged in his mouth so that his family could pour small amounts of water into his mouth. He could not talk but did move his eyes. He seemed to be in excruciating pain and rolled his eyes toward me as in a plea for help. Others gathered around him. I said "*Doo*" and walked away. Terrible.

He died that night. A few days later the village had a huge wake and I sat with the men and women who were drumming and doing wild animal dances and drinking *kai-kai*. It was a first-class Nigerian wake. I do not recall crying but I did get pretty drunk. The music was intense. They moved me from rhythm instrument to instrument every half hour or so. Each one had a different pattern. I would get it locked in and roll with it, then move to the next instrument. New pattern, more *kai-kai*. The daughter of a prominent village man walked me home, staggering drunk, reeling on my feet and laughing.

A few weeks later, the village held a traditional series of ceremonies for the elder and another man who had died three years earlier. A small boy and I were invited into a remnant of a traditional mud brick house to observe the ceremony of feeding the dead. That ceremony and others in Nigeria provided me with an ever-broadening concept of spirituality, reverence for life, and acknowledgment of death. But death was for others. I still felt indestructible.

TEACHERS TURNED SOLDIERS

As hostilities between the Eastern State/Biafra and the Federal Government were coming to a slow boil, two Nigerian teachers arrived at the college, both educated in England. I enjoyed their company immensely. They were Ijaw from Calabar, an ancient trading port on the southern side of Niger Delta. They were smart and fun. As they waited for their wives to join them, they filled their houses with friends and bar girls on the weekends. I joined a bit socially but declined most of the offerings.

The two teachers lived across the street from me. In the morning we would gnaw on chewing sticks and talk for half an hour or so. (I think my teeth and gums were better for that daily regimen than at any other time in my life.) At school, we joked around and I learned from them how to better communicate with students. Then, without warning both teachers disappeared. My cook, James, an Ijaw, told me they'd gone to fight with the Biafran rebels because the Federal Government had invaded the area near their hometown of Calabar. A few days on, James told me they had been killed defending an island in the Delta. Then James asked for final pay and told me he had to leave and go back to his village near Calabar. I gave him some money and said goodbye. I never learned his or his family's fate, but I suspect the worst. He was a good guy. He helped me a lot and I taught him how to cook western food.

MEN WITH GUNS

It was obvious that things were falling apart. But I was still a PCV with a low draft card number. I had my teaching and other work to do, notably a chicken farming project. I had received a box of Rhode Island Red chicks from England, and the students and I built a chicken pen on stilts to keep the rats and snakes at bay.

Such normal activities became irrelevant when the skirmishes between Nigerian factions escalated to an outright shooting war, which came to Warri just as my classes were preparing for their Higher School exams. It was early morning when two Biafran soldiers in camouflage pants and mismatched tee shirts entered my bedroom while I was still asleep. They had AK-47 type rifles. They marched me to the principal's office, where a well-spoken Biafran army officer calmly informed me the school was their new base of operations and I would have to leave immediately. With little more than my passport and a briefcase-sized suitcase I was escorted to the road. One soldier said rather apologetically that he had been to a school that had a PCV teacher.

On foot, interspersed with some hitchhiking, I made it to Sapele, a company lumber town a few miles north, carrying out an evacuation plan that had come in a letter to each PCV that very month. In Sapele, I met up with Patti and a small group of other PCVs also being booted out of the country. At nightfall we were directed to a huge, open-decked metal barge. A tugboat pulled the barge downriver in a moonless night. The tug stopped around midnight and tied off on mangrove trees. Our group of volunteers had no cover, no mosquito nets, and precious little insect repellent. One PVC, Mimi, shared her repellent with me, which seemed to only attract more mosquitos. Swarms of them flocked out of the mangrove forest to feed on American blood.

In the morning we were allowed off the barge and onto the tug. We continued downriver and neared the port where the Niger River met the Atlantic Ocean. There, we saw a small Piper Cub drop a bomb near a small Federal Government river patrol boat tied up at the dock. The patrol boat crew retaliated, firing its front-mounted cannon directly over our tug; it appeared to miss the plane entirely. The Piper Cub flew directly above our tug, dropping a second bomb near a large Federal Government troop ship on the opposite side of the river. Another miss.

We were in the middle of a live fire fight between the Biafran rebels and the Federal Government! Hundreds of soldiers on the troop ship were shooting over us at the plane, with the patrol boat shooting over us at the same time. We rushed to the side of the tug where we heard the cannon fire. Then to the other side to see the bombing of the Federal Government troop ship. The crew shouted for us to take cover, which I did not do until the little plane circled out of sight. The tug did not stop. It slowly proceeded along the coast to Lagos, where we were met by Peace Corps officials and sent to a college dormitory to rest and wait for our exit interview.

I was exhausted. Offered the opportunity to transfer to East Africa, I declined. My immune system was shot. I had boils all over my body, and had only recently recovered from a bad case of hepatitis. Having nearly been killed by malaria, I also suffered from tape worms, round worms, black fungus of the ear, and serial diarrhea. I had lost a lot of weight. My teeth were chattering during the final interview. I wanted out of Africa.

I wound up in Juan-les-Pins, near Antibes, France, studying French five hours a day for three months. A great place to get well and realize that I was not going to be able to save the world as a Peace Corps teacher. It was time came to go home, buckle down, and get serious about marine biology.

A Final Note about Tony Nwabaku

Tony had a burning ambition to study ethnomusicology in the US. We stayed in touch, and while he was a struggling student at Columbia University, broke as students often are, I was able to partially reciprocate his many kindnesses to a young, idealistic American with an appetite for risk who had been far out of his depth on arrival in Nigeria. From my small resources, I loaned Tony enough to procure visas and travel for his wife and children. He was desperate to remove them from harm's way as the Civil War continued. I am forever grateful to Tony—who, by the way, paid me back in full—for his warmth, talent, and wise counsel.

Nigeria on My Mind

In the twilight of my tenure on Earth, I can finally face the facts and memories of Nigeria, and remember those who died there during that troubled era. 'I wish their souls well. They taught me to better appreciate my life. I belong to a nonprofit, Friends of Nigeria, comprised mostly of PCVs, with a few other members from British and Canadian volunteer groups. Since Nigeria now bans Peace Corps workers, our ranks have shrunk dramatically and our group will soon either cease to be, or, hopefully, merge with former volunteers from West Africa, such as the Ghana group.

I left Nigeria in a traumatized state—mind, body, and soul—vowing never to return to Africa.

7.
STICK WITH BEER, THE WATER IS DANGEROUS

"Life is either a daring adventure or nothing."
— HELEN KELLER

Spending time in saltwater, as I did both diving and surfing, comes with an awareness of sharks. In my thirties I learned firsthand how complicated, physiologically robust, stealthy, and dangerous they truly are. But during what I think of as my "Indiana Jones" period, in Lake Atitlán, Guatemala, due to recklessness I almost died from nitrogen narcosis with not a shark in sight.

When Patti and I had flown into Guatemala City, returning from Chile, hostilities were rampant, driven by the lopsided wealth to poverty ratio of that potentially rich country. We spent the night in a central plaza hotel near the seat of government. At six a.m. we woke up to machine gun fire across the plaza. A senator had been assassinated. Political leaders were prime targets, but horrific events took place both in the hills and valleys of the interior and right out in the open in broad daylight in the cities.

Less worldly travelers may have deemed it prudent to catch the next plane home, but not us. Having been through the Nigerian Civil War and in Chile where things were starting to unravel after the election of the ill-fated Salvador Allende, a political assassination a block away did not faze us.

We went to breakfast and over coffee and eggs concentrated on how to connect with our hosts, Dave and his charming Nicaraguan wife Marta. Dave was a good friend from grad school, where he had been brave enough to drink our first batches of home brew, first beer, and then wine. These boozy concoctions were made in big buckets in the furnace room of our apartment building. Sampling and capping was party time. A few bottles exploded and made a huge mess, but generally our homemade beer and wine were drinkable at university parties.

Dave had a great laugh. We drank and ate pizza at the North Lake Tavern in Seattle, under the Montlake Bridge, swapping tales of our exploits in Third World countries. For his master's, he was researching cage culture of native Guatemalan species of fish as a subsistence farming project for indigenous people.

After breakfast in the capital city, Dave picked us up and we drove inland to the banks of Lake Atitlán, where he and Marta lived on a steep hillside on one side of a finger-like bay near the far end of the lake, across from the small village of San Lucas, in a red brick house with a red corrugated iron roof. Its rooms were small but the little house was elegant by local standards, with interior woodwork that displayed the skills and pride of local craftsmen.

❏ ❐ ❏

The community of San Lucas is almost totally indigenous; its hillsides are littered with obsidian flakes and pottery shards from thousands of years of farming by descendants of the Mayan Civilization. A family with roots in that ancient civilization lived next to Dave and Marta, in a small shelter, as caretakers.

I seldom saw the father, but I did see the mother, who had

several children; one of them, Pedro, was about twelve but looked much younger. He was an outcast and seemed to be malnourished. Convinced that Pedro had come from the seed of another man, the father made the boy sleep outside. Pedro got the least of the food and was short and thin. He followed Dave everywhere. Out of compassion, Marta slipped him food when other family members were not looking, walking a thin line between generosity and sensitivity to traditional cultural norms.

❑ ❐ ❑

As the four of us sat out on their open patio, catching up and enjoying local wine and beer, Dave filled us in on lake ecology and his research, conducted from a brown sixteen-foot fiberglass skiff with a center console and single outboard motor. Rock steps led down the hillside to a small floating pier where Dave tied the boat up. He talked about underwater features he could detect with the boat fathometer, and speculated about how the winds had capsized indigenous canoes on the lake, dropping cargo, in the form of pottery or weapons. Out of this jovial evening, a half-inebriated plan for an artifact recovery dive emerged. Little did I know that the "let's do it" attitude of young men egging each other on was about to put me in harm's way again.

Among the more troubling challenges of Dave's work was the erratic atmospheric patterns around Lake Atitlán, one of the most beautiful inland bodies of water in the world. That part of Guatemala sits on a geologic hot spot—tectonic plates move north, new volcanos emerge further south—and Lake Atitlán came into existence thanks to the collapse of a caldera from a long extinct volcano. The lake spans over fifty square miles and is surrounded by three majestic volcanos. Due to the swirling eddies of wind wrapping around the volcanos, the lake can be glassy smooth one minute, then suddenly covered with white-caps. This unpredictable wind pattern has a name in the local language: *Xocomil*, the wind that carries away sin. *Xocomil* made it necessary for Dave to have sturdy lines and heavy anchors to conduct his fish cage culture experiments.

On the skiff, Dave had a depth finder to mark out bottom contours, and he already knew of an underwater mountain that topped at about forty feet below the surface. This peak was covered with dense aquatic vegetation but not below ninety feet, due to the limits of the sunlight penetration necessary to support plant life. Below ninety feet there was only sediment.

Our assumption was that there was about ten feet of uncovered sediment on the side of the underwater mountain we could access on a deep, short, single-tank dive. We both knew that a dive deeper and longer would create a risk of an air embolism, which is often fatal. But we were gung-ho, hoping to find items that had fallen off canoes when indigenous villagers had crossed the lake. (Dave was reasonably sure that canoes had capsized from sudden shifts of the wind currents off the surrounding mountains, or through tribal hostilities.) Some items would be too deep for us, as our dive plan was only for a hundred feet deep, but Dave figured that the accumulation of artifacts over thousands of years of accidents made it worth the effort and risk.

The logistics were tricky, the water was cold, and Dave had only one wetsuit and one charged tank. But I was all in. We rented another tank and I decided to wear my white double-knit long underwear. Because of the planned depth of our dive we only had about five minutes, ten tops, to be on the bottom. We didn't expect to be in the water long enough for cold to become a significant risk factor.

Our plan was to tie strong plastic fish food bags to both ends of a hundred-foot rope, then dive to the bottom to grab some artifacts, putting them in a booty bag, which we would send to the surface by exhaling air bubbles into a float bag on the other end of the rope. Next, we would grab more artifacts, and repeat the procedure, with different bags. When we surfaced, we would grab the float bags on the surface and pull the artifacts up onto the skiff. Piece of cake! Fantastico!

We were both experienced divers with open water certification and Dave had spent many hours underwater in Lake Atitlán, observing fish in his cages and the behavior of native species of fish along the shore. High altitude dive tables were not available, and frankly we never considered the risks of scuba diving at a high elevation.

An Angel Named Pedro

As we gathered materials and loaded the boat, Pedro, the diminutive outcast, asked to go along. Why not? He was charming and helpful. The three of us headed out onto a still, glassy lake, where we easily found the lake's mountaintop on the fathometer, dropping anchor in about fifty feet of water, then letting out enough line to make sure the anchor stuck. Dave and I donned our gear and hit the water with deflated Buoyancy Control vests (BCs), sinking and swimming to the bottom immediately. Time was of the essence.

At ninety feet, we came to a sharp edge of green vegetation and benthic sediment. All sorts of things were sticking out of the sediment. I filled one bag with pottery and inflated the other bag at the end of the rope. The inflated bag went up and out of sight. On the muddy bottom, a wonderful pot with an animal face stuck out of the sediment, and I carefully placed it in my bottom bag, also grabbing two small dishes of pottery stacked together.

I swam down to inspect other items sticking out of the mud, which were surrounded by the beautiful color field of pristine blue water. But I was beyond our hundred-foot dive plan and unaware that I was now in a state of nitrogen narcosis, a nitrogen-induced intoxication of the brain. I was blissed out and going for the forever blue. A few feet farther down and I would have passed out. Recovery of my body would have been highly unlikely given the then-current technology of deep diving in Guatemala, and I would have been fish food on the bottom of a lake thousands of feet deep.

Suddenly, I heard an eerie sound and looked around and up and saw Dave pounding furiously on his dive tank with the butt of his dive knife. He pointed at the pressure gauge on the tank; we had very little air left. Since we were over a hundred feet deep, I inflated my final airbag and we slowly ascended, blowing out like crazy. We paused at the fifteen-to-twenty feet mark, but our air was low. I doubt if our dive decompression stop lasted even a minute. Sucking hard and trying to breathe when there is absolutely no air in the tank and you are looking up at the surface of the water is terrifying.

We kicked hard with our fins, holding onto our treasure bags. Our mouths filled with waves of lake water when we surfaced. We had not fully inflated our BCs. The normal way is to use tank air, but we did not have any more air in our tanks. Technically, we could have inflated the BCs by mouth, but we were in a life-and-death struggle, coughing and gasping, holding on to our treasures and exchanging frantic looks.

To make matters worse, in the brief time we had been underwater, the wind had come up, creating small whitecaps, and the boat was about fifty yards away! An impossible distance to swim with our heavy treasure bags. And we had another problem: we quickly found that the capacity of the float bags was not enough to bring our mud-covered treasures to the surface. Small streams of bubbles floated to the surface as the bags slowly sank.

Desperately, I dove down, grabbing one bag and abandoning the second one that was slowly sinking to the bottom, then kicked back up to the surface gasping. I got more water in my face and was coughing and kicking hard in confusion, looking at Dave with a sense of desperation.

Then the miracle happened.

Out of nowhere, the boat was by our side, thanks to Pedro's quick thinking. I grabbed the gunnel with one hand, holding my sole remaining treasure bag in the other, slowly bringing it up so Pedro could carefully pull my treasure bag into the boat. Dave did the same. Exhausted we slowly pulled ourselves into the boat.

Bit by bit, we grasped what had happened. The angles of both our dive and ascent had taken us away from the boat, which had also swung on its anchor and ended up even farther from where we had left it, due to sudden gusts of wind.

But Pedro saw our distress and had the presence of mind to throw off the anchor line, start the engine, and steer the boat to us without any training whatsoever. To me, he became a materialized manifestation of Divine Providence. By the time we returned to the little dock by Dave's house and presented our trophies to our women and took pictures, it gradually sunk in that without Pedro neither of us would have survived.

Earlier, swimming into beautiful blue oblivion with no thought of danger had felt so peaceful and right. And while underwater, I had no idea that my poor judgment would lead me to dive too deep, causing nitrogen narcosis. Thankfully, Dave's resourcefulness in using a hard metal object, the butt of his dive knife, to pound on his dive tank, made a loud enough noise underwater to get my zoned-out attention. It was only when we were in the boat that my mind cleared enough to begin to grasp the near catastrophe.

Among our other mistakes was the failure to calculate the length of the rope to allow for more than a hundred feet with knots and all. We also hadn't thought through the weight of artifacts covered by and filled with benthic sediment. And then there were the air leaks in the fish food bags.

On top of all this, we were ill-equipped and did not have an emergency game plan. When the same type of wind that had capsized countless Indian canoes abruptly came up, we almost shared their fate. To this day I still drift into magical thinking about having been saved over and again; it makes me feel protected that whether through Divine Providence manifested by the quick thinking of a boy barely in his teens, a companion more prudent than me (by far!), or my own genetically based survival instincts that always kicked in just when I needed them most, I am still here. Or maybe it was simply dumb luck again.

For years I sent money to Pedro, but Dave reported back that the family took it and the father just got drunk. Patti and I even briefly considered adopting him, which would not have worked out, since we broke up a short time later. May God bless Pedro. Maybe I had saved his life in another incarnation. He sure saved mine that day!

THE COMPASSION OF SHARKS

Few are familiar with Oman. And even some who know of it picture only barren rock and sand deserts like Saudi Arabia. Though that is true for much of the country, Oman, at roughly the size of California, also has coastal upwellings of cold, nutrient-rich water. Circulating wind patterns spin along the coast and push the Indian Ocean's warm surface water away from shore, allowing benthic water to reach the surface. This upwelling of water rich in minerals and especially nitrates provides essential nutrients for plankton, whose abundance leads, in turn, to plentiful populations of fish; and wherever there are a lot of fish, sharks abound.

Working as a fisheries scientist in over a dozen countries, I have never witnessed more fish than off the coast of Oman, where small tuna boil on the surface for miles in all directions. During data collection projects, we saw skiffs go out fishing for a few hours and come back loaded to the gunnels. Anchovy stocks were so ample that in half a day a skilled fisherman could catch a ton of them with a cast net, and toss them on the ground to dry and be used as camel food. The density of deep-water lantern fish, jellyfish, and anchovies was beyond anything I experienced anywhere else in the world.

My role in the development of Oman's natural resources spans three different stints over a decade. The first was in 1973, soon after a palace revolution. The heir-apparent son of the Sultan, fresh back from an education in Europe and Sandhurst Military Academy in the UK, concluded that the extreme poverty of the country flew in the face of fantastic oil, copper, and fisheries resources. When his father would not allow modernization, let alone a modern hospital, they argued, and the Sultan promptly threw his irreverent son in jail. Soon after, however, some friends from Sandhurst and the British intelligence service got him out and he shot his dad in the hip, sending the aging ruler to a hospital in Europe. In his absence, the son became Sultan Qaboos bin Said, who ruled the Sultanate of Oman for thirty years until his death in 2020. When I was invited to present some drawings of a planned fish meal factory to him, I blew it due to a beer and a jet lag nap. He proved to be a skilled and benevolent leader, bringing Oman from abysmal poverty to modernity.

Charles Black, a fascinating character in the world of American politics and espionage, did meet with the new Sultan, and promised to help develop Oman's fisheries resources. Mr.

Black brought a contract to Del Monte International, who hired me to get things rolling. At about the same time, the Chinese Communists initiated a revolution in Zanzibar, an island off Tanzania in East Africa. Recruiting Africans from the region, China brought them to the mainland for training and sent them back to Zanzibar in a submarine where they quickly overthrew the government.

A little history is necessary here. Before the British colonization of Africa, Zanzibar had been part of the Omani Empire. Under the British it was administered by English-speaking Omanis with deep roots in the country. Arabic Omani merchants had conducted trade along the eastern seaboard of Africa for thousands of years, using sambuks,[2] large wooden boat with lateen sails. They would sail down the coast on the winter trade winds, picking up riches from Zanzibar and sailing back home when the summer trade winds could push them north. The biblical reference to "ivory, apes, and peacocks" is linked to this intercontinental trade.

When the Chinese-trained revolutionaries killed, jailed, or expelled all Arabic people of Omani descent in Zanzibar, the new Sultan of Oman welcomed the refugees to help modernize his own country. Rashid and Mohamed Barwani, brothers who figure prominently in one of my most serious shark scares in Oman, were descendants of a family that had been part of the Omani-Zanzibar diaspora, first as traders in Zanzibar and later as government employees. When they were kicked out by the Communists, they had returned to the birthplace of their ancestors. Over the course of my three assignments in Oman, Rashid, who worked as my interpreter, and later as a senior government official, and Mohamed (both were accomplished sport divers

[2] I still have a replica of a sambuk vessel. In the 1980s such vessels were still being constructed by Omanis with traditional boat-building know-how, using bow and string hand drills, adze axes, and crude, handmade iron nails.

and fisheries scientists) became close friends.

I already knew that the plethora of fish in Oman was paralleled by a healthy shark population. That fact had been underscored while I was diving with Scott, a member of my project team, for spiny lobsters near the shore in rocky crags and coral reefs. Free diving for lobsters in Oman was like walking through a vineyard picking and eating grapes. They were everywhere. The local Muslims considered shrimp-like animals such as lobster unclean and never bothered to catch them.

Scott and I always threw back the gravid females with their masses of red and orange eggs. The males, however, went in the boiling pot. In a half hour of diving around coral heads and rocky outcroppings, we could catch enough lobster to feed everyone who happened to be around. There's nothing like spiny lobster, garlic bread, and cold beer for dinner!

On the day in question we were diving near the entrance to a bay, a half day drive south of the ancient city of Muscat. Working a shelf of rocks, we were picking up lobsters out of cracks in the boulders and a submerged escarpment. We wore gloves and were careful to avoid the moray eels that shared many of the crevices with the spiny lobster. Staying close to each other, we free dove along the rocky shore and quickly filled our yellow booty bags with fresh spiny lobsters.

Suddenly Scott was by my side, twisting the snorkel out of his mouth. "Did you see that huge jack swimming by me with a big piece bitten out of its tail, streaming blood?" Which meant sharks—and hungry ones. It was time to get out of the water. We were right up against a cliff in water a good thirty feet deep. So we turned to head to an outcropping where we could scramble onto dry land. But I spotted a sizable lobster in a crack about eight feet deep and could not resist a quick jackknife dive straight down into the rocky crevice. To steady myself, I held onto rocks with my left hand while arching my wrist around a big green moray eel. But the lobster slipped out of my hand, making a scrambling dash down the underwater escarpment with me inches behind it. I was pumping my fins as hard as I could, trying to grab it, to no avail. The lobster was lucky that day; it slipped into a deep set of broken rocks.

I was out of air, so shot up toward the surface. As I surfaced and gasped, Scott shouted, "Did you see that huge shark follow you down that wall?" I had not. It was high time to get out of the water. As in *now*! We swam back to back to a section of rocks and clambered out with our full load of spiny lobster!

After that, you'd think I would have known better. Not Bud! When Rashid and Mohamed Barwani, who had both been invariably kind and patient with my fumbling cultural and linguistic behavior, invited me to spear fish for a family party off a small island near Muscat, I was all in. Through them, I managed to learn quite a bit of Arabic and to see some of the country. It was on camping trips in the barren desert where I first fully experienced the majesty of the Milky Way on a crystal clear moonless night. I have never seen the night sky ablaze with stars like that night. The next morning I woke up to the friendly bells of grazing camels and goats.

For our dive near Muscat, Rashid and Mohamed had long-barrel, rubber-band-powered spear guns, which allowed for shooting big fish at a distance. Each spear gun had a long tether line connecting the spear to the gun. The process was to first shoot, then run the spear all the way through the struggling fish and down the tether line so the dead fish would be some twenty feet behind the diver, who would already be searching for more prey.

The Barwani brothers and I anchored in about thirty feet of water and put on our scuba gear, preparing to backflip into the bay. I exited first and dove to the bottom, clearing my ears, at which point I saw a brownish shark that was bigger than me and less than six feet away. It slowly swam out of my sight. I made a frantic dash for the surface, grabbing the gunnel and pulling myself into the boat, tank on, in one powerful panicky thrust of my flippers. I removed my mask and gasped, "Shark, *big* shark."

Rashid and Mohamed were still sitting on the gunnel. Rashid asked if it was a brown one. Lying on the bottom of the boat, head askew, I managed to get out a definitive "Yes." The brothers said nothing, then backflipped into the water from opposite sides of the skiff. I did not know what to think. I did not like being in the boat alone, so I dove back in after them. As it turned out, they had quickly shot several good-sized jack and rock fish, pulling them behind in about fifty feet of water. Fine enough, but within a few minutes I saw multiple huge sharks in every direction. Scared shitless, I powered back to the boat, waiting a half hour before the brothers returned with long strings of fish.

They told me that since the shark swam over me as I first went down, it must have been under the boat, and since I was not attacked they knew it was safe. (Besides, they had spears, while I had gloved hands and not even a knife.) This was all said matter-of-factly, as if the normal practice was to let the white foreigner go in first to see if the sharks were hungry. When I asked how they decided to come back to the boat, Rashid held up his spear gun and mimicked how he had been pushed backwards through the water by a big shark coming directly at him.

❏ ❐ ❏

Despite hundreds of encounters with sharks, they have never done me any harm whatsoever. Though one did bite the foot of a woman standing right next to me in shallow water. We had been practically shoulder to shoulder, talking in a foot of water near the City of Refuge, on the Big Island of Hawaii, when a shark about two feet long swam up and bit her on top of her foot. It left small teeth marks. There was some bleeding right at the tiny punctures, which stopped almost immediately. I made a big show of splashing the water and kicking at the baby shark as it quickly swam away. Why it passed over my foot and bit hers is a mystery I attribute to Higher Powers.

In my time as a charter boat captain in Hawaii, I caught hundreds of sharks and with few exceptions released them unharmed. That could possibly be a "bigger than me" thing, encompassing the collective energy of my relationship with elasmobranchs, which for me is one of compassion. Thinking they did not bite and eat me because I was compassionate is silly on one level, but there has been a lot of the "unusual" in my life, so I continue to hold that thought every time I go surfing or diving. Them, OK, but not me!

8.
THE KNIFE &
GUN SHOW

*"You don't need to be so fierce and bluffing
if you already know that I can't be intimidated."*
— JANE AUSTEN

When I first arrived on the Big Island of Hawaii as a thirty-three-year-old rolling stone, I quickly added beach bum to my résumé. A beach bum without wheels. Since there were no car dealers in Kailua-Kona, I took a bus to Hilo to check out some used car lots. When I cast my eyes on a beautiful, jet-black, tricked-out WWII style Jeep, I was in heaven. Simply put, I had to have it.

It had a chrome-plated valve cover and chrome headers off the engine and long, bright, shiny chrome-plated exhaust pipes on both sides. Chrome to spare! This under the hood brightness gave it a muscle car aura. It was open at the top with a big black roll bar. Someone had put a lot of love into that old Jeep. On a test drive, I heard a low rumbling sound. After removing the hubcaps on the twin exhaust pipes directly off the intake manifold, I drove it around the block again. This time it was outrageously loud. The salesman told me the former owner had replaced the standard engine with a powerful Mercury V4. That was it. Sold to the new guy on the island.

The first time I drove the coolest set of wheels I had ever owned into a gas station in Kailua-Kona, locals came over to check it out. I will always remember the expression on the face of this really cute local girl who looked under the hood with her boyfriend. There it was! The famous eyebrow flash Filipino women give a guy they find interesting.

At the time I was living in a sheet plastic geodesic dome in the Kona coffee lands and working as a deckhand on charter boats for cash. Every few days I drove my Jeep (the first and only vehicle I ever had an emotional attachment to) over to the post office to collect my mail, notably my unemployment checks. It was an important item on my schedule. Fishing in the morning, check the mail in the late afternoon.

The post office was where I met Pauly, under unfortunate circumstances, but let me back up for a minute to try to convey what had brought me to Hawaii and why.

After leaving the Peace Corps, I had an epiphany. To be of some use in this life, I resolved to get my PhD in fisheries science. Observing Nigerian children suffering from protein deficiency that led to disfiguring diseases such as marasmus and kwashiorkor had touched my heart. Their suffering handed me a mission—to give the Third World greater access to protein from the seas and rivers, through international natural resource development. And a couple more years at the University of Washington would put me beyond draft age.

With my sheepskin in hand, I spent six months in the bowels of the beast, working in San Francisco for Del Monte International, a Fortune 500 Company. As an educated heterosexual male in his prime, within forty-eight hours in San Francisco I had the keys to three good-looking women's homes! (Hey, it was 1972.) As well, I had a great salary by fisheries biology standards, and lived floating from hotels and temporary housing to other hotels and more temporary housing. I had a good time, but something wasn't right.

Working the system as best I could, I still missed the quiet of forests in the Pacific Northwest and the isolation associated with obsessive focus on my thesis project. Throughout my life I have been gregarious, happy, ridiculously charming, and engaging when the situation calls for it. But working for Del Monte made me standoffish. The job and the setting were not good fits. Del Monte's board of directors made my decision for me, by voting to get out of their traditional fish business and sell their canneries. As a freshly laid-off fish scientist, I decided to go fishing.

❏ ❐ ❏

So here I was on a sunny and balmy Hawaiian afternoon, at the post office to pick up my unemployment check, with the lot nearly full and people looking for parking spaces, picking up mail, and leaving at a steady, but glacial pace. I was pinned between cars and looking around for potential spots when I saw motion out of the corner of my eyes. Reflexively turning, I watched a rusty piece of junk slowly rolling backwards right at me. A rumpled, stocky guy was outside, comically trying to get back in it to put on the brake.

The guy dropped a package on the ground and had the door open but could not get in quickly enough. Holding onto the car door with both hands, he had one foot in the car and the other hopping backwards down the slope. At first the junker rolled slowly. Then it became a sped-up slow-mo nightmare. I had no opportunity to get out of its way as the stocky guy lunged at his car door one more time, without success. He stumbled, skipped a little step, and went down on the ground on his hands and knees. I watched in grimacing horror as the Rust-Oleum red bumper of the junker hit my lovely Jeep with a dull *thunk* smack on the front left fender.

The stocky guy lumbered over, apologetic—he had neglected to put the car in gear or set the emergency brake. I climbed out and along with several others inspected the damage. The dent in the left front fender came with a scratch on the shiny black paint. In the greater scheme of things, not horrific, except that it was a dent in my newly purchased women-impressing muscle car. I myself had caused much worse accidents in San Diego when I worked as a delivery driver. Well, at least the junker's rusty bumper had not so much as touched my Jeep's expensive chrome headers.

Horns were going off; I was blocking traffic. So I moved out of the way and got my first good look at the jerk who had let his piece of shit car roll into my beautiful Jeep. He looked a lot like his old Chevy, complete with its rust holes in the sideboards, a dent on the front fender, and faded paint. It was three colors: a faded light green that showed through; patches of yellow; and the harsh red of anti-rust paint over a rear fender that still had pullout holes where an unskilled body shop had drilled to try and pull out its many dents.

The stocky guy was dressed almost in rags. His shirt was half tucked in and hanging out on the side. Long sleeves had been cut off near the shoulder to allow for his short, massive arms to move freely. Strange, faded blue tattoos tried to decorate both arms. He was built like a fireplug, with the heavy body of a fat man; his legs were also huge. He was white, with a tinge of red in his short beard. His hair was a mess, with what looked like dust and bits of white debris, and the cuffs of his pants were cut off and had frayed strings hanging down. Laced-up black tennis shoes with holes on the side and a toe sticking out of one of them finished off his sartorial splendor.

I was pissed but holding it together. Initially I could not tell if he was a dirt-poor local or from the mainland. But when he talked, it was clear that he was not local. He was Coast *haole* all the way, a Californian by his accent. He begged me over and over not to call the police, saying he was working construction, putting up drywall, and would give me cash from his paycheck on the coming Friday.

Looking at this sad sack and hearing his pleas and promises calmed me down. Further, there was a reddish mark on his massive right hand, scabbed over, like he'd nicked it while working, and his ragged pants had white drywall mud all over them. So that part checked out. I started to feel sorry for this wreck of a man and his piece of junk. He introduced himself as Pauly and yet another time begged me not to call the police; he would cover all the repairs, he swore. OK, OK, I said, and got his phone number, address, and license plate number. Of course he did not have his driver's license with him; or an insurance card.

But I wasn't worried. He seemed genuinely contrite, and I believed he had a job. On top of which, I was inclined not to be too judgmental of the screw-ups of others, having made a mess of more than one thing in my own life. Besides, calling the police was low on my own agenda. I was smoking a lot of pot and growing plants with friends. Marijuana was a Schedule 1 drug at the time, and people were going to jail for years for possession and transport of small amounts of *pakalolo*, as they called it in Hawaii.

My partner, Robbie, and I were growing plants at hiding places scattered all along the Kona coast hills. Plus, I was gaming the system by crewing on charter boats for cash while collecting unemployment. Not exactly a bank robbery, but still quite illegal. All in all, Pauly's pleas fell on the sympathetic ears of a new guy in town not inclined to make enemies. Who knew who this mismatched brute knew or was related to? And what kind of harm could they do to me? Even though I was almost six two and 175 pounds, this muscular, foreshortened version of the Incredible Hulk could easily crush a tall skinny guy like me.

On the spot, still at the post office, I formed a plan. I had been hanging around with Reff, a musician, mechanic, and gun dealer who seemed to have connections to the nefarious Aryan Brotherhood. Reff had also set up a vehicle repair business with Robbie, my *pakalolo*-growing business partner. I figured I could go to their shop, use their tools to pop out the dent, and spray paint the scratch in an hour or so, and the whole effort would be less than a hundred dollars. Smoke a joint with Robbie, play a few tunes with Reff, collect my money from Pauly: it was going to be a no big deal event. Pauly and I shook hands. The plan was for me to fix up the Jeep the next day, then on Friday meet him at the construction site a few blocks away so we could settle up.

Well, on Friday I ended up on a charter that took longer than expected. We had hooked a big black marlin on the way back to the harbor, a relative rarity in Hawaii. At first it had been a slow day, no action at all, and we were trolling with small, shiny, jet head lures in about forty fathoms of water (240 feet deep), figuring maybe a Spanish mackerel or *ono* as they are called in Hawaii, would bite. But then a two-hundred-pound black marlin came up chasing our small lure with its mouth wide open and bill slashing at the air. We could see the top of its powerful tail movements creating a wake as it rushed at the lure, and I slacked off the drag and let the lure drop into the marlin's gaping mouth. When the marlin turned to the side, I increased the drag to set the hook, and when the pole bent, signifying the fish was hooked up, I slacked the drag on the reel and let the fish run. Fishing line screamed off the reel as the marlin ran and jumped.

The angler, although a complete novice, sat in the chair as I told her to, and we got the fighting harness on her and gave her the pole. But after a long day drinking in the sun, she started crying; she could not follow my instructions, and it didn't help when her husband shouted at her. I finally got her out of the fighting chair and got her husband in the fighting harness and the pole in the gimbal. Anyway, a lot of line had gone out and it took nearly a half an hour to get the marlin onboard.

It was almost dark when we tied up at the harbor that Friday. Then came the photos and other formalities at the dock, and cleaning up the boat. Long story short, Pauly was not at the construction site when I arrived. Construction work generally knocked off by four and it was closer to six.

Over the next couple of weeks, I kept trying to find Pauly, and in the process found out he'd given me a bogus home address. But I was working long days on the boats, happy to have a job and trying to keep it, and evenings were for music, getting stoned, tending our crop, and chasing after tourist woman. Finally, I made it over to Pauly's construction site again on a Friday afternoon, but he had just left.

By now, though, I had his real address from his coworkers. This is where things got very strange. It was a late weekend afternoon when I got out of my cool Jeep and climbed the steps to a little old house and knocked on the door. No answer, so I sat down on the front steps. The house was probably fifty, maybe seventy-five, years old; it was a faded, light green, and the cracked wooden steps were painted white. My fuse was growing short. We have a deal, I thought. We shook hands. I did the repairs. I need the money—and he has to pay me!

So I sat there fuming for about twenty minutes in my Kona charter boat deckhand uniform of thigh-length swim trunks, a blood-stained tee shirt, and cheap flip-flops. Then a funky car pulled up and a big woman got out and came toward the house with a bag of groceries. She was about forty, with long black hair, and wore tight black capri pants and a loose multicolored blouse. She had serious arms like she did physical labor. At first I thought she was Hawaiian, but as she came closer I saw that she was white, with a sizable Italian nose and generous breasts that jiggled as she walked.

When she asked what I was doing there, I told her I had come to get reimbursed for a car accident. She shrugged and said she didn't know anything about that. She climbed up the steps, unlocked the door, and went inside. As I was pondering the situation, Pauly drove up in his beater. Carrying a brown paper bag of groceries and with a stubby digit through the finger hole in a gallon jug of red wine, he said, "Oh, hi." Sort of nonchalant, like an old friend had dropped by. He walked past me and started up the stairs.

Immediately I was on my feet and right behind. As he opened the door, I was in lockstep with him, my flip-flops almost touching his heels as he stepped through the doorway. He turned, tilting his head a little, but with no angry facial expression and not saying anything, as if he had forgotten. So I explained that we had a deal and he needed to pay up.

He looked me up and down. I was an uninvited guest in his home. He told me to sit on the couch across the room. His voice was steady. Still no anger, no flush of color. For a long few seconds we unselfconsciously sized each other up. After which he looked up at me again, tilting his head, and shrugged and walked away.

I did as he said and sat down on an old brown, food-stained, sagging couch. When he went in the kitchen where the big woman was, I assumed he was going to get his checkbook or cash. He stayed in the kitchen a long time. I figured he was explaining to her about the accident and our deal not to call the police, and getting the money together. I took in my surroundings; there was nothing on the walls and no other furniture than the dining room table and two chairs. The springs in the couch poked through the cushions no matter where I positioned myself.

Voices filtered out of the kitchen. I heard Pauly call the woman Doreen. Doreen brought out two plates and big water glasses. No indication that I was being invited to break bread with them. Shower noises suggested Pauly was not focused on getting my money. Doreen brought out the gallon jug of red wine and poured the two water glasses to the top. A few minutes later she brought out a large pot and shoveled piles of spaghetti on the two plates. Glancing over at me with a blank face, she then went back into the kitchen. Moments later she brought out a long-handled cooking pot and scooped spaghetti sauce on the piles of noodles. Turning to look at me squarely, she took a long gulp of red wine, never saying a word.

When Pauly came back, he barely glanced at me and sat down to eat. It was painfully obvious that there was not a third plate or glass on the table, so I just sat on the couch watching them. As Doreen refilled the two water glasses with red wine, they talked softly between themselves, looking over at me from time to time. I continued to sit there with my hands on top of my thighs.

After about twenty minutes and another topped-off glass of wine, Pauly carried the dining room chair over, the chair he had been sitting on as he ate and drank with Doreen. He plopped it down directly in front of me so that his knees were about a foot in front of mine. He was uncomfortably close but not touching me. Remember that by this time he had probably poured a quarter gallon of red wine down his throat. Though he was clearly lit up, he was not staggering or clumsy.

Pauly then leaned forward. Staring at me with his small

bloodshot eyes, in a firm but not hostile voice he asked, "Why are you here?" It was a genuine question, as if he needed to be reminded. I laid out the whole event—his car rolling down the slope in the post office parking lot, the damage to my precious Jeep—adding in his pleas that I not call the police and our hand-shake agreement that he would cover the repairs. Now I was here for my money. I showed him the receipt from Reff and Robbie's garage.

He looked at the bill for a long minute, like he was trying to read it through wine-clouded eyes. Finally he said, "Doreen, bring me my knife."

I was still leaning back in the couch, like Mr. Casual, but thinking this was not good. My legs were not crossed and my hands were on top of my thighs. In truth, I was more curious than concerned, though there was no denying that things had turned very weird. Somehow, I did not bolt for the door, al-though the potential of this ending badly was slowly dawning on me. Pauly could harm me. Hell, his huge better half could beat me to a pulp.

In response to Pauly's request, Doreen came out of the kitch-en and disappeared into what I assumed was the bedroom. She came out holding a substantial hunting knife in a leather sheath with long brown leather tassels. I knew this kind of weapon, from my hunting days in the Cascade Mountains, where I had shot a big white-tailed buck in the neck and field-butchered it into manageable pieces with my own Bowie knife. Pauly's knife was over a foot long, with a blood notch and a bone-cutting serrated top edge. It had a handle made from knarred brown elk-horn, with a curved silver butt on the end and a copper-colored bolster. It was impressive.

Pauly started taking it out of the sheath, slowly, and then with a flourish pulled it completely out and held it up in the air in front of me. Like Mr. Cool, I said, "Nice knife. I used to have one just like it when I hunted deer in the mountains."

Now he started a little game of lightly passing the knife from one hand to the other and looking down at it and then back at me. I was still leaning back in the couch with my hands free, but I adjusted myself slightly, with my palms and little finger still on the top of my thigh but the other fingers free and closer together. At that moment it was not at all clear that I was being threatened. An observer could have easily conjectured that this was simply two guys talking about hunting knives. Which was not the case at all.

The knife continued to pass from hand to hand slowly, after which he started to toss it from one hand to the other more quickly. That little quick toss movement was anything but casual, and for the first time I sensed the real possibility of violence. But as I believe my ancestors did in times of mortal danger, I somehow stayed relaxed and started talking. A genetic inheritance I am convinced.

I smiled and said, "That is just like *West Side Story*."

Pauly paused but continued moving the knife around. He showed no interest in discussing movies. After about another minute of this knife show, he put it back in the sheath.

There was another pregnant pause, broken when he turned in the chair and shouted a little too loudly, "Doreen, bring me my gun." She was near the kitchen door, watching us with her arms crossed. There was no need for him to shout. But he *was* a bit drunk and probably wanted to scare me.

Doreen went back in the same room and came out with a large, black, long-barreled .45 Magnum revolver. I knew this type of gun. Big gun, big bullets. Still, I remained seated, leaning back in the couch as she gave the Magnum to Pauly. With my hands now at my sides, I remained completely calm as if I were talking with an old friend about his gun collection.

Pauly obviously loved that .45. He smiled, rolled the cylinder with a quick whipping motion, and flipped the cylinder open. I could see there were no bullets in the chamber. Then he snapped the cylinder shut and slowly at first, then quickly, brought the gun up and pointed it right at my forehead. Even though I knew there were no bullets in the cylinder, this was absolutely a threat. His face changed, his eyes squinted as he stared at me. Most ominously, he puckered his mouth, squeezing his jaw so much that his lips went from a straight line to a zigzag. That look has lingered with me to this day. I suspect that is the very face that came over him when he had actually killed someone.

I surrendered to the moment. The worse the situation grew, the more relaxed and low-toned my voice got. I went into deep relaxation mode. I wish I could tell you that I was saying to myself, "Stay composed. Keep talking to distract. Do not show fear. Keep talking." But I can't. I was on automatic pilot. It was all just reflexes.

"That is one nice gun, man!" I told Pauly. Mind you, he was still pointing it directly at me and the end of the barrel was inches from my forehead. "I bet you could do some damage with that gun and hold off the police if they were coming for you," I went on, turning my head to look out the window past the end of the couch. Maybe he thought I was trying to psych him out, but that was not the case. In retrospect, I think that perhaps by turning my eyes away from his—looking out the window as if there were actually police coming for him—I became less threatening to him.

He turned his gun toward the window. I was not directly challenging him; not even sweating or breathing hard. Pauly continued looking out the window in a sort of alcoholic fixation. After a few long seconds, maybe he remembered something. I do not know, but I am guessing he was considering scenarios of gun battles past. Regardless, he put the gun down in his lap.

Then he barked out the most amazing thing. "Doreen, bring me my hat." I remember being taken aback by this outburst. She went into the bedroom and came out with a tall, black, shiny top hat, like bankers wore in the 1800s. I had never seen a real top hat up close. This one was made of felt and was in perfect condition. Doreen handed it to Pauly and he put it on with an animated flourish as he stood up and gave her the gun.

The Knife & Gun Show was over. He reached for his back pocket. I was still on full alert—but he pulled out his wallet and picked out his Friday paycheck from the construction company. "You owe me the difference." He spoke very lightly. No more threats, just taking care of business.

"Yeah, I don't have that kind of cash on me" is what stumbled out of my mouth. "I can write you a check but my checkbook is at my apartment."

"Let's go!" is all he said.

With only a nod toward Doreen, Pauly accompanied me to the door and we went down the steps like old friends. When we got into the Jeep, he sat at first, and then stood up holding onto the roll-bar. As I pulled away from the curb and picked up speed, he took off his hat and waved it in the air, whooping it up like he was herding cattle. He was obviously having fun. We went to my apartment, where Robbie and Reff were smoking pot and listening to music.

Pauly waited in the living room with his hat on and they all just stared at each other. I quickly wrote a check for the balance and give it to him. He looked at it and got serious for a moment, asking if it was good. I said I guaranteed it and that he knew where to find me. We shook hands and said our sincerest *mahalos*, Hawaiian for thank you. I drove him back to his place and we chatted like old friends telling fish stories and lamenting the price of good weed.

When I got back and filled Robbie and Reff in, their first response was laughter. Then they made fun of me. Then they raked me over the coals for bringing a gun-toting thug into the house, a thug who now knew where they lived and that they had *pakalolo*. I shrugged it off. Hey, I had my money.

A few days later, at the post office picking up my mail, I glanced over at the bulletin board behind glass. There was Pauly's picture! He was on the FBI's Most Wanted list! The physical description, the height, the weight, the short reddish beard—it was all there. I stood in open-mouthed amazement. The wanted poster described him as armed and extremely dangerous. He was associated with a notorious biker gang involved in a lot of violence. There was a big reward.

So his knife and gun had probably seen action in gangland incidents. He was a violent man who may have done harm to innocent people or even murdered someone. But with me he had been smart enough to know the limits. Since he was on the run from the FBI, if he pissed me off or hurt me, he would draw attention and likely get arrested again. Pay a small bill and move on seemed to be how he worked it out in his mind.

He was even a bit classy in his own strange way. And he had a woman who could go toe to toe with him and take care of him to boot. Not to mention that his knife and gun were clean and first class. He had probably scared people off on many occasions by playing his "Bring me my knife, bring me my gun" game. But his bluff didn't work like that on me, and apparently he'd decided I was OK, that I had balls, since I could not be dissuaded by a gun pointed at my head.

The next morning I woke up feeling exhilarated. I had faced down a knife and a gun—and my karmic connection with Pauly was clean. How and why I stayed relaxed under duress, however—with Pauly and in many other dangerous situations—would take years to fathom. It was only at the age of eighty, rereading about my great-great-grandfather George—notably how in a remote forest clearing in the early 1800s he confronted, and talked and talked for hours to, a group of Native American renegades intent on killing him and his two companions—that I began to postulate the influence of my epigenetic history. The DNA of my bloodline had been helping me all along!

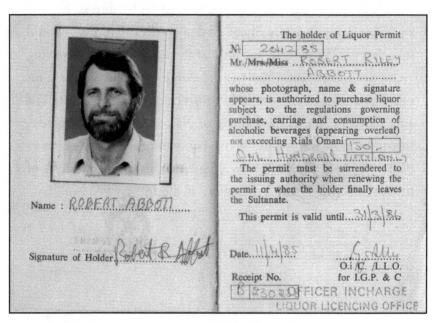

License to buy alcohol in Oman

Data collecting at the fish market, Oman, 1985

Aunty Gyi doing a psychic healing on my spider bite rash, Rangoon, Myanmar, 1987

Presenting the ADB prawn fisheries project results, Myanmar

Presenting the Tarawa Lagoon Management Plan, Kiribati, 1990

Holding an eel trap, with Tarawa Lagoon project team members

Paying homage to Charles Darwin in the Galápagos Islands

A fun day fishing in Cabo San Lucas, Mexico, 2023

Working with the team placing a radio transmitter tag on a large female elephant, South Africa

Of course, the road washed out, Costa Rica

With my daughter Michelle at St. Andrews golf course, 2022

Golfing with my son Tom keeps me healthy

Zochi Young demonstrating the conversational aspect of tai chi push hands

The hotel in Dubai that caught on fire with me on the 48th floor, 2022

Teaching TRANSFORMATION tai chi at the
Lighten Up Retreat, Costa Rica

Priscila Soares, documentarian for my tai chi book
TRANSFORMATION and the Lighten Up Retreats

Kathryn Remati, cofounder of Lighten Up Retreats, a meditation trainer, Costa Rica

Performing music with a message, where people can sing along — one of my pleasures

9.
PARADISE
SQUANDERED

"It is important to expect nothing, to take every experience, including the negative ones, as merely steps on the path, and to proceed."
— RAM DASS

This part of my life reflects the ethos of a time and place when substance abuse was common, and I was both pining for and denying adulthood, living as a postadolescent adrenaline junkie. Retrograde, sexist attitudes and amoral behavior I have long since outgrown and repudiated cannot be left out of this story.

Four years later I was still in Hawaii. Things had gone my way, thanks to an unexpected windfall from a real estate deal in Seattle, and I was living out a dream few get to experience as the owner-operator of the *Pisces*, a thirty-foot charter fishing boat. I was even president of the charter boat association!

In the best of times charter fishing is not a lucrative profession—the hours are long and the income sporadic. But while I had not apprenticed on fishing boats, my training as a marine biologist put me in a position to assess and cross-reference data to advantage. A charter boat operator needs to go where the fish are, so I read real life oceanic currents, wind, tides, and temperatures like others read the stock market trend lines. It was my job, but I loved it.

Known as Captain Dr. Bud, I was the charm-to-spare guy with standing in the community. But I was also pushing forty, and during long lonely hours in the tuna tower of the *Pisces* scanning the ocean for indications of fish, I caught myself daydreaming about having a family, most especially after a happy one had chartered my boat. I was envious of the richness of affection and encouragement between couples and their children. But when not daydreaming about domestic bliss, I remained true to my hard-earned reputation as a free-and-easy opportunist with female tourists seeking a vacation fling.

Maybe it was my active social life and propensity for alcohol and recreational drugs that led me to turn a blind eye to political and mega-economic trends, even as business began to fall off, then kept getting worse. (When I did not have a charter, I would generally go the commercial fishing route to pay the bills, but that also had its ups and downs.) Add in the advent of Asian long liners, and the tip of the iceberg I was about to hit assumed Titanic proportions.

RED FLAGS IGNORED

Then an omen came along, in the form of a serious ethical lapse—although I wasn't paying attention. In short, vanity and substance abuse combined to almost bring me to ruin when a repeat customer, an American businessman who was sometimes with his wife, sometimes his mistress, chartered the *Pisces*.

The *Pisces* needed work, but the client had cash—and I needed the cash to get the work done. So I went out anyway, despite badly needing a replacement carter key in the drive train between the engine and propeller shaft. These relatively small strips of metal are made of case-hardened steel. There was one in Hilo, but not enough time to get it before the client arrived, so I found a soft iron, galvanized nail to use temporarily, and we headed out to fish along the shelf north of the airport.

Using live bait we hooked up a huge blue marlin, upwards of 700 pounds. Somehow she[3] threw the bait, but the hook stuck in the hard bony edge of her mouth. Then she did this amazing thing, swimming right up to the stern of the boat and flashing her colors. My stalwart deckhand, Steven, and I looked over the stern in the crystal-clear water and shook our heads in agreement. We were not going to try to gaff and bring that monster on board quite yet.

The charter sat in his chair reeling in slack line as Steven and I decided that this big mama was going to have to run. I skipped back to the helm and gunned the boat. Line screamed out and she jumped. She jumped clear of the water, over ten feet long, right behind the boat so we could see her full body in profile, lit up like a Christmas tree in blue, red, and yellow, with flashes of green. Phosphorescent skin cells she used to signal her readiness for mating or a fight. Her back was pitch black. The belly was shiny white. Her dorsal fin flipped erect. She was magnificent. She was angry. She was trouble.

She ran just below the surface, leaving a wake like a submarine. I backed down the boat, following her as my charter tried to reel in his line. This went on for half an hour or more. Finally, the poor client's skin broke and trickles of blood showed on the handle of the reel and the hand grip on the pole. The reel had 130-pound test line and Steven had set drag to maximum, which did not slow the massive marlin down at all. After some time the charter was not able to reel or even lean back in the

---

[3] Blue marlin above 400 pounds are called "girls"; at that size, they are all biologically female. Which could be a case of a mixed population of protandric hermaphrodism (males changing into females as they grow).

fighting chair. He leaned over his reel, exhausted. The big fish leaped clear of the water again, even as the charter's wife got motion sick and vomited into the small green trash bin filled with beer cans and boat debris.

Then came my comeuppance, payback from my corner-cutting ways, in full force. The soft galvanized nail in the drive train broke and the boat stopped moving.

I pulled up the hatch cover and jumped down into the hold and saw the parts of the broken nail on the bottom. It had made a poor substitute for the carter key I'd neglected to buy. Quickly I installed another nail, my last one. If the second nail broke, we would be stranded, fifteen miles offshore, and drawn into the windy channel between islands with sick and bleeding passengers. Somehow, the second nail held. I wrapped the fishing line around a boat cleat. She jumped again, and the line broke. She jumped one more time and was gone, sparing me, barely, humiliation and possibly worse. On the way to the harbor, we caught a 125-pound yellowfin tuna and I called it a successful day, got the carter key, and ignored the red flag.

Hooked in a Blink

A month later, I fell in love at first sight, as romantics would have it. It happened as I was crouching on the bow of the *Pisces*, fixing the anchor line to the chrome-plated cleat. My attention was drawn to happy laughter that seemed to dance across the water, the laughter of a young woman. I glanced toward shore and my gaze landed on a tall, long-haired blonde in a group of men and women on the sundeck of a funky beach house alongside the rocky shore of Keauhou Bay, on the Big Island. The blonde had her back to me.

I had anchored on the bay for years, and tourists like these at nearby hotels and rentals would routinely hire me to take them fishing for big yellowfin tuna and blue marlin a few miles offshore.

The young woman stood up straight. She was striking, with a narrow waist, a thin back strap below her shoulder blades, and a big yellow bow tied behind her neck. She threw back her head, laughing again, and turned slightly to the side, revealing a yellow and black polka dot bikini top. Perhaps to amuse the women, one of the men jumped at the base of a coconut tree, as if trying to get a coconut that was well out of reach. She laughed some more, a trilling, giggling sound that sent chills down my spine. I actually shook my head and shivered as I fixed my gaze on her with a tunnel vision as focused as that of a predator eyeing prey.

> As established by research into brain function, coupled with studies in behavioral anthropology, courtship, and mating behavior, we are largely driven by genetic programming. When a young woman displays her availability via genetically orchestrated readiness vocalizations, such as a sharp high-pitched laughing sound, and a young male hears it, a response is unleashed in him. He surveys his options.

Captain Bud was instantly smitten, and though not particularly evolved in any in such matters, was not about to let his atavistic urges take over. Which still left plenty of options. A hundred yards from shore, I stared, chin down, sizing up the group, even as I washed down the boat and went over ways to meet her, despite my current look: a tee shirt with fish slime and blood all over it from the day's fishing. So I took off my aloha-yellow and green tee to wash and hang on the helm to dry, and sat on the fish box for several minutes, chewing on the arms of my sunglasses with my hands resting on top of my thighs.

Brushing back her hair, the young woman turned slightly to the left, revealing tight curves above and below the waist; she wore yellow-patterned capri pants. Pure and simple, I had to meet her. So I put a two-pound skipjack tuna in a plastic bag, tied the bag to my leather belt, confirmed my fish knife was secure in its sheath on the other side of my belt, and lowered myself over the stern of the boat into the water, executing a breaststroke to the rocky shore near the beach house. Then, barefoot, I gingerly climbed the riprap and lava rock bank and stepped onto the grass beside the house, standing slowly so as not to startle, while simultaneous picking out the alpha male in the group.

I introduced myself and pointed out my boat moored just offshore, easing into my well-rehearsed spiel about fishing and the big blue marlin found along the Kona Coast. I allowed that I had heard them having a good time and felt drawn in, but had not come empty-handed. Pulling open the plastic bag, I presented the two-pound skipjack to the big man closest to me and offered to prepare some fresh sashimi for their party if they could show me to the kitchen.

> The young male's introduction to a new band of hunter-gatherers might involve offering food to the dominant male(s) to acquire tentative access to the group. This practice, in millions of variations, has gone on for millennia as men seek mates outside their extended families.

Up closer, the object of my fixation was even more striking. Her long legs were accentuated by the framework, lines, and dots of the bikini top. As I sized up the group, asking a few practiced questions about where they were from and how long they were going to stay on the Big Island, I realized how seamless my rap had become after seven years at the trade. Talk up the dream. Get the money. Do the best you can to catch a big fish.

The big man introduced himself as Bolt, as in nuts and

bolts. He jokingly said he turned wrenches on large equipment, hence the nickname. He neglected to say anything about the "nut" that went with the bolt, but his satisfaction in describing himself said it all. Bolt informed me that he and rest of the group—his wife, Casey, his sister, his brother-in-law Tim, and Tim's girlfriend Sally—were down from where they lived now, Alaska, for at least a month. Home was also dark and cold a lot of the year: they all came from the same small town in northern Minnesota. Apparently, there was no work there. Tim stepped forward and said, "We know cold and long dark days. But Alaska is too much." Now it was November and ice was everywhere and construction work was miserable and nearly impossible.

The object of my interest was Bolt's younger sister, Maja. She had tagged along to Alaska, and now to Hawaii. Maja was smashing, like a cat-walk beauty with Scandinavian features. I hoped my tongue was doing the talking and not just hanging out.

In their kitchen I used my stainless-steel knife to prepare sashimi on a much-used cutting board. I cut off the head and removed the guts, then split the fish down the middle and removed the main bones and skin to yield long strips of flesh that could easily be cut into small edible pieces. Rendering a skipjack or small yellowfin into thumbnail-sized strips of fresh raw tuna sashimi was an everyday activity for me. I had filleted hundreds of them over the last decade. The process was quick, efficient, and not particularly messy. Often I prepared it right on the boat to entertain charter families during the long wait for a marlin strike.

As I worked, I chatted about the thrill of watching spinner porpoises leap high in the air, and of finding schools of skipjack a mile off Red Hill, just south of Kailua-Kona. This particular skipjack, I explained, had been used earlier that same day as live bait without success. Of course, I bragged about how the man who chartered my boat had landed a large blue marlin the day before in the same spot where we had caught the skipjack my new friends would soon be eating.

Bolt and his gang had money or they would not have been able to rent this little house right on the water, and I was consciously hooking them like so many fish; hustling tourists was my profession. Maja, who had unconsciously prompted me to climb the rocks, was momentarily forgotten, having become noticeably quiet once I appeared on the scene. No more high-pitched laughter and giggles. She stood tall, chin down, moving her head side to side and shifting her position, so she always had a view of me. I noticed, however, that she seemed to position herself so as to always have someone between us.

At the time, subtle assertiveness was my style. Fish stories proved the right bait for most men, while jumping spinner porpoise stories worked better on the women. And there I was, feeding a group of total strangers, flexing my social skills, and showing off my toned legs, flat belly, and broad shoulders to Maja. In my charter boat period, I was usually half-naked anyway, in a swimsuit or shorts.

Whenever I glanced at her, Maja ever so slightly turned her head away, tilting up her chin, exposing her neck, arching her back, changing her posture in a way that pushed all my buttons. The movements were so faint that only instinctual, flash observations let me know she was at least subconsciously interested.

> *Innate, non-verbal, courtship signaling in human females is an area of robust scientific inquiry. Many universities have departments of sexual studies focused on the biology and behavior of such interactions. Formal names have been given to specific courtship behaviors, among them erotophilia, a personality characteristic related to the response to sexual cues.*

The two older women seemed to catch what was going on, as evidenced by their eyebrow-flashing each other with suspicious movements of the corners of their mouths, along with telling sidelong glances and head gestures.

The layers of the scene I was witnessing were comical. When the meal was ready I knew that the reaction of Bolt, the alpha male, when tasting my food offering, would signal the degree of my acceptance to the group. He stuck a toothpick into a slice of sashimi, dipped it in a small cup of soy sauce, and turned his head away as he mouthed, then swallowed it. He took a second small piece and wiped it over the wasabi, then into the soy sauce, and turned away again. When he turned back to look at me with a smile, it was clear that I was in! He grew talkative and proudly spoke of Maja, who had been working as a sign painter in Anchorage.

These party people were all very white and still dressed in Alaska street clothes, except for Maja. Bolt, curiously, wore a plaid, thin cotton, long-sleeved shirt. I began to notice that they were drinking heavily and had been for hours. Empty cans of beer on the ground and an open bottle of vodka on the deck table informed me that they were definitely out to have a good time. The two older women in particular were a bit wide-eyed; they started dancing erratically to some heavy-beat rock music, coming back to the table, swishing their bodies to the rhythm of the music for more sashimi.

Fresh sashimi and cold beer are a treat anywhere in the world. A symphony for the taste buds. Bolt's wife Casey tossed back her head and placed a strip of sashimi on her tongue to show how brave she was, swallowing the strip of meat without chewing. Then she ran around the kitchen laughing. With her mouth wide open, I noted her rotten teeth and gums. Noticing the poor condition of her teeth, I reflexively stood up a bit straighter. My first yellow flag warning sign.

Then I noticed that Bolt was tanked: he stabbed at a piece of sashimi with a fork and missed his target. In his alcohol-induced neuromuscular fumbling, the fish fell to the floor. When he bent forward to retrieve it, a hypodermic needle fell out of his shirt pocket onto the floor. First Casey's bad teeth and erratic, jerky movements, and now the syringe. I realized suddenly that they were meth heads, methamphetamine addicts. The Big Island was notorious for its "crack whores," men and women who would do anything for a fix, even pick coffee berries for the farms that produce Kona coffee beans.

I did not outwardly react to this fresh disclosure. But I went on high alert. Drug addicts generally meant trouble. Not that I was particularly judgmental, since I myself was both an alcoholic and addicted to marijuana, and occasionally used speed or meth to stay awake during long boring moonless nights fishing for valuable bigeye tuna.

Compared to the others, Maja was reserved. She quietly used a fork and tongue-tasted a bit of the meat, re-examined it, and then took the whole piece, dipping it in the sauce and biting into it, holding it in her teeth for several seconds as the rush of green mustard, salty soy sauce, and fresh fish meat flooded her lingual and olfactory sensory glands. She nodded and smiled at me with a slight lifting of her eyebrows. There it was, the instinctive eyebrow flash. I had gotten the "Interested!" signal. The eyebrow flash is just one of the behavioral communication tools common to primates and humans that probably are antecedent to verbal communications in our evolutionary history.

Up close, Maja turned out to be younger than I had originally thought. The skin around her face showed her to be almost a teenager. Her breasts were small and she had thin legs, broad hips, round buttocks. I suddenly wanted her, needed her. Something serious was going on here.

After more small talk, about Alaska, construction, and big bucks for heavy equipment contractors, Bolt leaned into me and came out with their real purpose for this trip, whispering that what they needed up there in the Alaskan winter darkness was some Kona Gold. He confided in me that he wanted to take back a big suitcase of it. He talked like we were old drinking buddies. And yes, he had the cash, he assured me.

I cautioned him about flashing money around Kona, which had a well-earned reputation as a hotbed of gangsters. The "Kona Mafia" competed with rivals from Hilo, and there had recently been a gunfight on the Kailua-Kona boat pier. Furthermore, the Japanese Yakuza were in open warfare with the Oahu-based Korean mobsters that ran the bars in Waikiki. Not to mention the law to contend with.

Although I knew growers in the Kona hills who were into music, my policy was to absolutely avoid buying my personal stash from anyone I had not known, and known well, for a long time; plus, I never sold pot, to anyone, ever. Give it away or say no. With all this in mind, I joked to Bolt that I would lose my skipper license if I got caught. I told him how just a few months back the DEA had swept the charter fleet clean of obvious users in a massive sting.

The hour grew late, and I needed to leave, but not before trying to rope them into a day charter, and if that was a nonstarter, at least getting Maja to go commercial fishing with me. I told them I would aim to catch a large yellowfin but that sometimes when fishing for tuna we would hook a big marlin. Looking straight at Maja, I said they had to be dockside at 4:30 a.m., sharp. To increase the probability of hooking up a big tuna, I had to be five miles offshore at first light.

Then I left the way I had come, gingerly, barefoot down the riprap before plunging into the Keauhou Bay like Aquaman.

With the powerful free-style stroke of a surfer, I swam to the dock instead of back to the boat. Climbing up onto the wooden pier, I saw the group of five standing on the lawn looking at me. Maja waved. Casey turned and seemed to reprimand Maja about waving at a stranger. I smiled.

> A brief meeting and withdrawal after introduction and food offering constitutes a pattern locked in a male's genes from a million years of courtship interactions. Young males had to interact with other tribes in order to obtain mates and complete a reproductive cycle.

I drove up *"Mauka"* (mountain, in contrast to *"Kai,"* the sea) toward the town of Captain Cook, to get a bird's-eye view of the ocean. Stopping on the hillside lookout, I studied the direction of the Langmeyer lines, which suggested that I would be fishing a bit south the next day, five miles out from the coastal landmark of Red Hill. Relaxed, I rolled a joint of Kona Gold, took a deep draw, and savoring both the intake and the smoky exhalation, reviewed the few words spoken by Maja, while picturing her every movement. At home, I cooked fish from the refrigerator, having given away my dinner. Maja dominated my thoughts, and my dreams that night.

CONFIRMATION COURTSHIP

At 4:30 a.m. sharp, Maja showed up at the dock, alone. She looked nervous but lovely under a wide-brimmed, floppy hat tilted at a rakish angle, with the same big bow in her hair that she had worn at the beach house. An oversized, baggy, Alaska day jacket borrowed from her brother topped her bare legs. Small plastic yellow flowers poked up between her toes in brand new flip-flops.

Casey and Sally had taken her to the nearest hotel tourist

shop and demanded that she get the hat. They were worried about her Alaska pallor. Were they also displaying genetic behavior of their own?

> In many cultures, girls and young women are offered to prominent men in order to bind clans together. This pattern is seen in European, Middle Eastern, and Asian cultures, and is the subject of much drama. In the primate world, mother bonobo chimpanzees may direct their male offspring to have sex with other high-ranking females.

Bolt's gang had a mission, even though they did not talk about it much. Buy a suitcase loads of *pakalolo*. To do that they needed to move around, maybe get some introductions. Find out where the danger lurked and make arrangements. What better way than to send out the girl to seduce the big local guy? Later, as we got to know each other better, Maja told me Casey had explicitly instructed her along these lines, telling her to "make yourself noticeable, make him think you are fair game. Flash it. You got the stuff, girl. Move it. Tease him a little but not too much."

Despite my attraction to her, I managed to greet Maja professionally with a handshake, and to ask about the others. She spoke softly, saying they had partied late and could not get up so early, they were all still jet-lagged. She also said she could only stay out until noon since they were booked for a tour of Kona coffee farms and an evening luau and hula show.

What she really wanted was to see porpoises and maybe catch a big fish. Laughing between phrases, she spoke through a toothy smile, a little jumpy but direct, with even a bit of child-like animation and a flick of white showing just below the hem of the coat. She dropped her head sideways, still smiling, and looked up at me, piercingly, with intensely blue eyes. She was surprisingly bold, which only upped the ante given my "going to get lucky" state of mind.

I took off my long-sleeved tee shirt and flip-flops and ran down the pier as was my custom, diving into the water and swimming out to my charter boat. I had the powerful strokes of an accomplished swimmer and reached the boat in seconds. Stepping on the rudder, I put a toe in the exhaust pipe and pulled myself up over the transom in one motion. I fired up the engine and released the anchor line and deftly backed the boat up to the dock, tossing Maja the stern lines.

She laughed some more, mouth wide open, moving the rope from hand to hand, not knowing what to do. Then she did, sort of. She dropped back her head, displaying her neck and rolling her eyes to show the whites. She was in good spirits as she tugged on the ropes. She was really pulling me in. Her signaling behavior sent a rush of testosterone through my bloodstream.

In fishing lingo, her antics constituted a strike if not a hook-up. I jumped onto shore and took the lines from her hand and showed her how to "figure-eight" the lines over the dock cleats. We did it together, Maja copying my hand movements as we tied up simultaneously on opposite cleats.

> Synchronized movements are common courtship patterns seen in many animals and especially birds. In humans, head bobbing, nods of agreement, and dancing are synchronized movements affirming readiness to proceed.

As I went through the preliminaries, lifting the hatch cover to inspect the bilge and oil and fuel level of the big Cummings diesel engine, we chatted. She told me her first name was an archaic Swedish derivative of Maria and that her family name, Barnstead, was from a long line of Swedes from Minnesota where her parents still lived. Her father's grandparents were originally from Sweden and her mother's people were Danish and Icelandic immigrants who had come over in the early 1800s. Speaking with a bit of a northern Midwest accent, she pronounced her first name with a soft "j," which made it sound almost like Ma'a.

After carrying two hefty bags of chip ice from my pickup, I went into the forward cabin to bring out four large, big-game fishing poles. I handed them to her one at a time and told her to put them in the rod holder holes on the sides of the boat. She energetically carried them around the fish-fighting chair and set the rods in place. She seemed happy to help and was telling me more about herself. After high school, she had gone to Alaska following her brother. She was an artist and told me some details about her job in Anchorage at a small sign painting shop. Winter was a time to leave Alaska, and she was traveling with her older brother and his friends because she had broken up with her abusive airplane pilot boyfriend. Her disclaimer was not lost on me: she was available.

Maja shrugged off her breakup and the abuse, saying, "Well, at least I got to join the Mile High Club." The hint that she was sexually active and ready for anything piqued my curiosity. I made a point of asking her age. Nineteen. My caution came from the fact that there were lots of fourteen-year-olds in Hawaii who looked much older and lived bed to bed. Rape is indefensible, but even consensual sex with a minor is illegal. I knew from common knowledge that there cannot be any penetration of a female unless she clearly consents and is at least fifteen, the unofficial age of consent in Hawaii.

Maja helped me get the boat ready. She had tied back her hair into a folded ponytail, moving fluidly, finding her way around the fish box and fish-fighting chairs. I looked straight into her eyes and smiled as I handed her a fishing pole and with a toothy smile told her where to place it in the rod holder on the side of the boat.

"Here?" she asked, holding the rod above the rod holder hole.

"Yes! Put it in!" I laughed when she leaned forward and turned sidewise to me, looking over her shoulder.

After firing up the engine, I asked her to throw off the anchor line and she did, seeming at ease as she squatted and sorted out how to pull the loop of the anchor line from the bow post. With her back to me, still squatting, she turned and looked over her shoulder, holding the anchor line in one hand, the other pressed on the shiny bow post. I was triggered and thought that she must know she was sending me some serious signals.

"Drop it in the water to the side of the boat, then come back here to steer," I said. She looked back coquettishly and tossed the anchor line and small float to the side.

A sense of collaboration and easy communication settled over us. I was enjoying our easy banter and her enthusiastic and sassy attitude. Slowly I steered the boat out of Keauhou Bay, dropping of my shoulders in relaxation. Her competence somehow gave me a rush of lust. Once outside the entrance, I thrust the throttle lever full speed ahead and we were on our way across the flat glassy ocean of the Kona side of the Big Island and straight out to the open sea.

Three volcanic mountains soaring almost 10,000 feet above sea level protected the lee side of the Big Island from the blustery trade winds that battered the Hilo side. While the windward side of the island was often rainy and nearly always had a light breeze, the Kona side was dry and often had no wind at all for many miles offshore.

A flat calm ocean and the throb of the powerful Cummings

diesel engine made it seem like we were flying across the water. When I asked Maja to steer the boat straight out to sea, she sat confidently at the helm as I instructed her and showed her a point of reference (a small boat barely discernible in the soft morning light). When I barely brushed my hands over hers to show her something, did she intentionally lift a finger to touch my hand?

When she focused on the dot-like outline of the small boat, I knew she was attentive and comfortable steering, so I returned to the stern and set up *ono* lures. We quickly caught two big *ono*. These relatives of Spanish mackerel are excellent eating and I could always sell them to restaurants for cash.

It was a good day: a few money fish on ice, a pretty woman with me on her mind, my own business, a charter boat. Another sun-splashed day in Kona. I was giddy with gratitude. On a primal level, you could say I was demonstrating that I was a provider. On another, a very happy guy!

Maja seemed more than a little stunned by the intensity and brutality of how I dispatched the fish. As I turned on a water pump and washed down the deck, I did not talk much while I pulled off my tee shirt and scrubbed the fish blood and slime off with a brown long-handled brush. This was definitely not trout fishing in Minnesota.

Farther offshore, I noted some flying fish launching and gliding just above the water. In response I changed the lures to bigger jet heads, with two hooks on each lure. Their skirts, of soft blue and white plastic, gave the impression of flying fish. Two lures were set far back on the outriggers and two were run close behind the boat, just in back of the prop wash foam line.

Maja watched me set the tuna fishing gear without my wet tee shirt on. I was aware that she was looking at me. Those days saw me at my physical peak! I was lean and my muscles showed beneath my tan. Long, unkempt, wavy hair flowed down the back of my neck. She looked at me some more, then back out at the ocean, a silly, happy smile washing over her. Apparently lost in thought, she let the boat turn, and I called to her to go straight toward some clouds on the horizon and two other boats. She made an exaggerated wiggle in the helm chair, sat up straight, and shouted "Aye, aye, captain."

Now I started to share my story with Maja, interlaced with information about the island, oceanography, and the receding shoreline landmarks that helped orient my fishing strategy. I told her about Captain Cook Bay and the Red Hill volcanic cinder cone; both helped me to assess oceanic fish behavior in relation to subsurface island features hundreds of feet deep. I told her about my PhD in marine biology and how I'd dropped out from academia and business to do what I needed to and loved the most, go fishing.

While I spoke, she fussed with her hair, and as the day warmed up, she opened her baggy coat, revealing a white and yellow tourist tee shirt tied in a knot at her waist and snug white short-shorts. Beneath the tee shirt was the same polka-dot bikini top that had caught my interest before.

It was time to look for spinner porpoises, so I invited her up into the tuna tower (more commonly called a crow's nest), a strong aluminum-framed lookout perch some twelve feet above the main deck, providing an unobstructed view for miles around. This viewing platform was small and almost cage-like, with one seat and controls for steering the boat. Up there, we were practically shoulder to shoulder and ours occasionally touched.

From the platform, I could see the ocean's surface, seabird behavior, small floating objects—it all told a story to help predict fish distribution. In general, fish distribution is patchy, not evenly dispersed. I was looking for anything that would suggest aggregations.

Spotting some small boats moving along with a pod of about a hundred spinner porpoises, I pointed them out to her. Spinner porpoises often stay a few miles offshore in a large pod that can be seen up to several miles away; periodically one will jump and spin and crash into the water. They mainly feed on deep water squid and lantern fish, at night. During the day they sleep, at least half of their brain asleep. Looking into her eyes from time to time, I chatted about porpoise reproductive behavior. They play and mate, a lot: social sex, group sex, chase-and-play sex.

At the time, courtship and mating behavior in other mammals was a hot topic in my informal readings. I was fascinated by such patterns in human cultures too, and by unconscious triggers for arousal and courtship behavior in humans. Looking into Maja's eyes, I smiled broadly as I described porpoise ecology and mating behavior. She smiled a lot too but did not ask questions. She turned away or went blank when my boat chatter on oceanic ecology and the business of catching fish flowed into our "getting to know you" conversation. This was all getting intensely personal, with biological courtship drives in play irrespective of the words.

After a few hours chatting and fishing, Maja and I came down from the tuna tower. She had been thrilled to see the leaping spinning porpoises, and I also felt her physiologically reacting to me. I definitely wanted to touch her. At one point, as she quickly turned to watch a porpoise execute a series of jumps, she brushed her elbow against my biceps, letting her elbow linger on my arm. I did not react. My surface demeanor remained all business.

Back on deck, we had soft drinks from the ice chest, then I returned to the helm seat and steered with one hand, keeping an eye on the fishing lures and scanning for any sign of birds or surfacing schools of small fish that might indicate tuna. She stood near me holding onto the countertop. I had not yet put my wet tee shirt back on after catching the *ono* and cleaning up. It was draped across a chair back.

I asked her to rub sunscreen on my back and she squeezed the long orange bottle of 40 FPS, leaving a trail of cold white sunscreen across the top of my shoulders. Then she rubbed it in, at first with only her right hand, and then with both hands moving up and down, then in circles across my shoulders. Awkwardly she put some more sunscreen on my lower back. When I offered to rub sunscreen on *her* back and shoulders, and suggested she take off her tee shirt, she pulled off her floppy sun hat and untied the knot at the base of her tee, crossing her arms and pulling the tee up and over her head. It was almost funny the way she did it. Then she fussed with her hair. I could not help looking at her chest.

She stood up straighter, looked away, smiling with a soft "thank you." A bit formal but I caught the edge of her smile. I again offered to apply sunscreen for her, but she declined, saying she had put some on earlier before coming down to the boat.

Sitting in the helm, I steered, scanning the horizon and glancing back at the fishing lures shimmering in the stern waves, then at Maja, then back out across the horizon. We spoke calmly and I noticed a change in her behavior. She seemed to be talking a bit more about herself and had both hands up, fiddling with her hair. She was still standing right next to me, but fidgeting, swinging her shoulders, arching her back, as if thrusting out her small chest and sticking out her rump. She smiled more, looking directly at me. Then she reached her left arm across her chest and patted her right shoulder, displaying a genetic courtship marker of her own, as her piercing blue eyes left me gape-mouthed.

> Such let's-get-it-on behavior is seen in gorillas, chimpanzees, and bonobos, a sort of I'll-rub-your-back-if-you-rub-mine signal.

I had been around and was familiar with biologically driven behavioral expressions of sexual interest, although I was never sure if women always knew what they were doing and why. What I did know was that when those types of courtship gestures were made, my advances were seldom rejected.

There it is again, I thought, as she used her right hand to rub the top of her left shoulder anew, a clear invitation to touch her back. So I made my move, reaching out and pulling her to me with my free hand so that we were hip to hip. I leaned down and kissed her gently on the lips. Lip-locked, she did not let me finish the kiss. I undid her bikini top and a lot of fumbling, passionate, groping and kissing ensued.

Then everything stopped—what was that sound?—when I looked back toward the stern and saw the corner pole bent, with line screaming out. Then I saw the marlin jump.

"Fish on!" I shouted, abruptly shifting gears. All business, I pulled back the throttle to slow the boat to idle speed, set the wheel for a slow turn to port, and pulled Maja out of the helmsmen chair, pointing her toward the fish-fighting chair. We were both nearly naked. I slipped her arms through the fish-fighting harness and pulled the rod out of its holder. In small steps, I put the rod into the fighting-chair gimbal and handed her the rod, telling her to lean back and reel in line as she bent forward. She leaned into the task, hair askew, half-naked, red-faced. She leaned back and then quickly forward, reeling in line for nearly fifteen minutes to bring the marlin up to the side. I grabbed the leader and brought the marlin up to the side of the boat. It was completely dark.

The bright, flashing colors of a mad, very live marlin were warning signs that there was fight left in it. A lit up, alive, and angry fish could jump or lunge ahead, dragging my hand or even breaking it as sometimes befell even experienced big-game fishermen. When gaffed, a "green" marlin can jump and land in the boat, injuring people. Ever since a fellow fisherman lost an eye that way, I had been cautious.

This fish fought to its death; it was rigid as a board. Jumping and making furious runs to escape had exhausted all its energy reserves. Being pulled toward the boat with the hook, when added to the pressure of the fishing line preventing normal respiration, was too much. The fish died of asphyxiation and lactic acid cramps.

Holding the leader with my left hand, I told Maja to hand me the long-handled marlin gaff. I swung its hook end across the back of the fish and pulled it toward me, running the steel through its dorsal musculature. It hardly moved its tail at all. I dropped the leader and held the gaff line and waited for any sign of vitality. Still holding the gaff line, I asked Maja to hand me the aluminum baseball bat with a rope loop on the handle end. She did and I threaded my free hand through the loop, and with a large sweep of my arm rained the bat down on the white spot on top of the marlin's head. The spot was clear of skull bone, allowing light to stimulate the pineal gland near the marlin's brain. I used the white spot as a target to inflict a quick, no question about it, kill. In no way did I want a 175-pound marlin making a last flurry of tail beats as I was hauling it on the deck.

Next, I asked Maja to put the rod back in the holder and help me with the fish. She unsnapped the fighting vest and strode proudly, still half-naked, to my side and gave me a big kiss on the cheek before picking up the rope.

The jumping marlin, I soon realized, had been like a beacon in the night. Charter boats from miles around came to see the action and let their passengers watch the commotion while they waited for their own fish to strike. In the background, my CB radio was a cacophony of Hawaiian Pidgin English jokes. The word was out. I looked up to see four other boats circling; one of the captains and some passengers had their binoculars locked on Maja, not the marlin.

Captain Bud was definitely in his element: catch a big fish, catch a pretty woman. As stated previously, I had a reputation, if one I did not particularly savor, and I did not relish how this event was unfolding. In terms of natural human courtship rituals, the new mate is eventually introduced to the community—just not this soon, and not this way! Grabbing the CB's microphone, I said simply, "Her name is Maja." Obviously I would have preferred to introduce her to the fleet in a more appropriate manner.

What happened next is something I would never have imagined. Maja strode out from under the shaded canopy of the main deck, and in all her topless glory stood tall with her hands on her hips to face each leering boat. In my mind at the time, she was marking her territory. I saw her as a tough young woman, signaling to about a hundred onlookers, "Deal with it. You have your story. I got my man. My man. Not your man." I broke into laughter and felt a rush of emotions deeper than lust. She was not yet twenty but whatever she was doing, she knew her onions. Ours is a competitive world and there are times you need to express fierceness.

> Competition between females for access to mate choices is innate and common in many species, including ours. Women reflexively tend to mark their mate, especially in the eyes of other woman. The ring on the left hand, insistence on a very public declaration (such as a wedding), or even an out-and-out hair pulling slugfest—all reflect the drive to mark status and a mate.

The CB crackled congratulations from several boats, followed by ribald jokes about what kind of bait I had used. There were also charmless references to a small reddish fish that colloquially referred to the pink color of a woman's vagina. Additional comments touched on clothing standards for the fleet. These comments were broadcast for miles around on the radio band used by all the fishermen along the Kona Coast; this led to some raucous, half-intelligible CB chatter, broken English, and interrupted transmissions as the fishermen joked about my reputation with women.

Maja, no doubt, heard a lot of the comments, and even if she missed the meaning of some, she changed her behavior and looked at me with a sidelong, straight-lipped expression. She seemed to be taking note that I had not deflected the chatter. Where was my defense of her? She became intensely quiet.

The unwanted attention and her amazement at her own behavior seemed to confront her full blast. What was I doing, she must have asked herself, suddenly self-conscious of how she had outrageously flirted with a man she hardly knew, and with just short of humiliating results. She tersely reminded me she needed to meet Bolt and his crew for the luau and Hawaiian entertainment show. The hour it took us to get back to Keauhou Bay was strained. We were both alternately lost in thought, embarrassment, and amazement. There were moments of tenderly intertwined fingers and a few kisses on her cheek and forehead, but her mouth was not available. Much as I might have wished, I could not just stop the boat to try to talk over our situation. Besides, her family schedule and crossed arms made it clear that any discussion was premature. Still, somehow, my behavior, if not my actions, seemed to revolve around protecting Maja. Strange, I thought.

When we reached the dock, I backed the boat up to it, and

after tying up the stern lines, gave her a friendly hug and kiss on the cheek. I would come by her place tomorrow afternoon, I said, if that was all right with her. She murmured that tomorrow they were going on a drive to Puna and South Point, and left the dock on foot for the beach house. At the top of the steps, she stopped and turned back, raising her right arm a little to give me a small wave. Then she was gone, almost running away and disappearing behind a grove of palm trees. Long after she was out of sight, I watched that spot, looking at the tree trunks where I had last seen her.

Loading the fish into the back of my pickup, I poured the rest of the ice over and covered them with an ice-soaked burlap bag. The drive to the icehouse was like a century of lost time as I flashed continually and repeatedly about the beautiful too-young girl I had just seduced and everything she had said and done.

The bad vibe on the return trip cut like a knife. I had a huge crush on Maja, which left me dumbstruck, hoping I had not completely blown it. Her youth and smile broadcast an image of perfect, radiant health. Was that the mythical aura I had seen? I felt I could walk behind her, protecting her and doing whatever was necessary for her happiness, forever, mesmerized by the swing of her hips. Could she be the base to launch me into family life? Mind you, I did not even consider differences in age or education; my thinking was fixated on a ridiculous kind of "does she love me? does she not?" obsessive compulsion. Was this actually a love thing? Which at the time was foreign to me; I simply did not consider love a factor driving my life.

Still and all, after one day together on the open sea I couldn't help but fantasize about us as a couple. That long, luscious hair, her clear skin, her long legs, and wide hips—was it all advertising for her ovaries? Was she considering me to become the father of her children? If so, the primal part of me wanted the job!

All these thoughts crisscrossed in my mind (and loins), despite the fact that I knew hardly anything about her. What I did know was that she had left her abusive former boyfriend, as well she should have. That told me she was someone who made her own calls, demanded respect, and had her limits on what she would put up with.

A School of Trouble

A few days later Maja brought Bolt and the gang down to the dock. She led them like a line of ducklings, one stumbling after the other. They were unkempt and totally wasted. Staggering, stoned, walking hazards, they giggled, their eyes out of focus, their speech disturbingly slurred. Which might have been funny at a party but was not remotely amusing on a boat with lots of sharp things everywhere. When they offered up magic mushrooms and Kona Gold, plus cold beer and Jim Beam whiskey, I realized they were completely baked—at eight in the morning!

In a quick convoluted side conversation, referring to the sour ending of our first boat trip, Maja informed me, "You owe me one." I agreed, and helped Bolt and company get on the boat, slowly; first, I took their hands and guided them up the steps on the stern, then helped them down, gingerly holding one or both hands to get them seated. Subliminally I must have known that this was all a very bad idea. But I needed to pay the bills, so I had to go fishing anyway, and why not take them along?

Maybe I had been overly generous in inviting Maja's brother and extended family but I definitely wanted to impress her— and Bolt. After all, he was part of my future imagined family!

Once I got the clear of the harbor and steered the craft out to sea—assisted by my now-experienced deckhand Maja, who doubled as a teenage mother hen, ordering her brother and Casey to sit down—my next task, before ascending the ladder into the tuna tower to scan the horizon for boat and jumping porpoise, was to set the lures.

But what was Bolt's stake in all this? I wondered. He seemed to see me as a pal or a liaison to the grower community—assuming his drug-addled brain could actually form an idea. While the gang enthused about looking for spinner porpoises, I reminded myself that I needed to reel in at least one yellowfin to make my nut. OK, I needed more than that: I needed Maja to love me. To be proud of me. On that score, I took pains to make clear that I was in charge, the captain of the ship.

> The genetic drive to display in front of a potential mate highlights the male ego's need to gain status and attract attention. The potential mate's tribe members have their own drivers—to gain the respect of the male seeking admission to their tribe, and to advance status in the pecking order of the local territory. For her part, the future mate must demonstrate motherly leadership to show her potential "husband" that she can handle such a situation.

What followed was a panoptic demonstration of risk-taking behavior: Maja trying (to no avail) to keep her crew of wasted idiots in line despite their colossal displays of vanity; and Captain Bud too enamored of Maja to do his job—herding the cats who were his charges that day.

There was another factor in play, which only underscored my lack of judgment. To save money, I had stupidly (and potentially illegally) dispensed with the services of Steven, my experienced deckhand, and would have to be everywhere at once if necessary.

Dismissing all of these consideration, I lit a joint—if you can't beat 'em, join 'em—as soon as we were out of the harbor, and after about an hour, some miles off of Red Hill, I chewed a small handful of magic mushrooms Bolt offered me out of a small jar. He testified to their freshness; they had collected the mushrooms the day before in the cattle ranching area at South Point. They joked about going through barbed wire fences and how Casey got her blouse caught in the wire and tore it off and went "shroom" picking topless.

In those days, the late 1970s, the psychotropic effects of psilocybin mushrooms were poorly understood. In a general way, the magic or spiritual part of psilocybin and the hallucinogenic effects of peyote cactus buttons were known to a few, mostly through the writings of Carlos Castaneda and the community surrounding Baba Ram Dass, and through experiments with LSD at East Coast universities. But seeking deep personal insights or spiritual experiences, or treating troubling psychological problems was not part of the scene in the Hawaiian fishing community. Magic mushrooms were just traditional party drugs.

I had taken an assortment of drugs, although I preferred marijuana, and had only eaten a few magic mushrooms at gatherings of locals on the Big Island; mushrooms cooked in a fruit pie or chewed up, chased with scotch and a lot of joking around was the ticket. The high, in my experience, enhanced emotional issues. Sex on a few mushrooms had brought me to tears.

That morning, I knew I was eating more mushrooms than I ever had before at one time. But Bolt egged me on. I washed them down with beer.

> The need to conform is itself a driver. Further, trying to impress in such a situation is akin to strutting or implying that a man would risk his life for his mate or offspring. When a man makes such signals, it can trigger subconscious neural hormonal pathways in the potential mate's mind and body.

Maja had only one mushroom and washed it down with a giggle. She followed me up to the tower, where she sat beside me with her shoulder against mine or against my leg when I stood up to look around. Once, as she lifted her arms over her head to adjust her hair, she brushed her hand against the front of my shorts. I became semi-tumescent and laughingly looked down at her with a smile that hid nothing of my desires. She tilted her head as if questioning whether she should do more of the same.

> The much-studied bonobo has 98 percent of the same DNA as we do. Bonobos are "randy," and will have sex in just about any situation. Females at times will use sex to calm a situation, relieve stress, and increase community bonding.

The mushrooms were starting to take effect and the Kona Gold was heady stuff all on its own. The combination of the two, plus beer, was in no way a wise move on Captain Bud's part. Periodically, I started to laugh out loud at nothing, emotionally rushed with the beauty and vastness of the ocean all around. I whispered words of affection to Maja.

No more whispers. "Fish on!" I shouted, and pulled back the boat throttle, slowing the *Pisces* to an idle and spinning the wheel hard to port before shimmying down the ladder. On the deck I saw that Bolt was smashed. It was a comedy of errors to witness this large man trying to put on the brown leather fighting harness. First backwards, then upside down. His brother-in-law Tim was hardly more competent. After Tim helped Bolt stand up, they lunged toward the center fighting chair.

It was difficult to suppress laughter at the sight of them trying to get Bolt seated facing the stern. He moved like a plastic figurine bobbing in the air, trying to turn the handle of the fishing reel, even as Casey lunged for the side of the boat to vomit. The excitement and quick jerky movements of the boat was too much for her.

With Bolt finally in a safe sitting position, I grabbed the outrigger pole and started reeling to take up some slack line. I gestured for Tim's girlfriend Sally to sit in the second fighting chair and just hold the pole and reel in a little at a time. She promptly leaned forward and vomited on the fishing reel before leaning to the side and finishing the purge with projectile vomiting on the deck and her feet.

The action began nonetheless. The first fish was at the boat in minutes, a small oceanic *ono*. I gaffed and carried it, tail flipping rapidly, still on the gaff, to the fish box, ordering the others out of the way. "These fish have razor sharp teeth, so sharp that if they bite, you will not know it until you start bleeding!" I warned them.

Soon after, we had a second small *ono* in the fish box. I reset the lures and started fishing again almost immediately. Seeing nothing in the water to mark where more fish were, I threw a seat cushion over the side of the boat as an area marker. Then I scrambled back up into the tuna tower, knowing there had to be other *ono* in the area; in open water they travel in schools. From the tower I searched for anything floating. I was sure there was a floating object in the area.

Then I spotted a few pieces of sugarcane in a Longmire line. Longmire lines, which accumulate debris such as sugarcane, planktonic organisms, and small fish, are the result of converging currents that generally run perpendicular to the main current. Big fish like *ono* will follow the Longmire lines looking for small fish to eat.

Sugarcane grows on the Big Island and is processed on Maui. Plantations cut the long stems and truck them to a barge near Hilo. The barge loading process always results in a few stalks dropped in the water, and the Hawaiian trade winds push the ocean currents around the Big Island to the Kona side. As I headed for the sugarcane stalks, two more reels went off and the starboard outrigger clip snapped.

Three fish on, accompanied by the frenzy of inebriation. I became a whirling dervish, raw energy in action, all shouts and orders, while moving equipment and praying that no one would get hurt. Somehow I got three silvery fish on board myself.

Maja had stayed up in the tuna tower and was leaning over the rail watching it all. Finally, the pounding of tails in the large ice-filled fish box subsided and I started the seawater pump and squirted water on the deck to clean up the blood and fish slime and vomit.

After a few more passes, I recovered the floating cushion and sat in the deck-level helm seat. An increasing level of calm fell over the boat. The Cummings diesel rumbled to a steady beat. The revelers were all asleep: Bolt sprawled out on the deck, Tim in the second fighting chair, and Casey and Sally head to foot on the fish box.

Maja was standing by me at the helm when the mushrooms kicked in full-bore just as the adrenaline rushing through my veins washed out. Suddenly I was overcome with fatigue so profound I had difficulty moving my arms. My eyes would not stay open. My head listed from side to side. I thought I was going to pass out in the helm chair. Maja was the least impaired of the lot of us, but I could hardly speak to ask her to steer the boat south back toward Keauhou Bay. We were far enough offshore that the Big Island was just a brownish blur on the horizon, and she had no idea which direction to steer.

I could, though, still make out the faint reddish cinder cone of Red Hill, and Maja could follow my gaze and shaking finger pointed at the faint vertical red line on the horizon. When I was sure she could see it and had the boat pointed in the right direction, I slumped down the two steps into the forward cabin, grasping anything solid to support myself, and lay down on the blue cabin cushions. I fell asleep instantly.

The hallucinogenic effects of the magic mushrooms were intense and fascinating. A woman in a long, white gown appeared before me in dreamtime. I had seen statues of her and was positive it was Quan Yin, the Southeast Asian Goddess of Mercy. Fishermen in Vietnam prayed to her before every fishing trip. With a smile, as if whispering in my ear, she said, "Go to Maja."

Opening my eyes, I was completely refreshed and calm. Yes, I thought, good idea. I should go and start a life with her. I was ready to settle down. I felt a love for her that I had never felt before. I climbed the two steps out of the cabin and saw Red Hill directly in front of the boat. We were about to run onto the rocks at the base of the crumbling volcanic cinder cone!

Perhaps out of boredom from steering the boat in a straight line, Maja had fallen asleep too and slumped to the side, almost falling off the helm seat! I lunged for the helm and yanked it hard to the left, looking with terror through the clear water at the rocks just a few feet below. An ocean swell seemed to lift then set the boat down. I felt a shudder in the helm as the rudder touched an underwater boulder. Mercifully, the forward motion of the boat carried us free. The prop did not touch rock. We were safe, if by a mere fraction of a second. One more instant and the boat would have crashed into the rocky shore at the base of Red Hill.

I was in shock. None of Maja's family and friends had any idea of our narrow escape from disaster that could have proven fatal to some or all of us. Barring that, there would still have been the loss of my boat and my skipper license, and quite possibly jail time. I was shaking with adrenaline. "Oh my God, oh my God," echoed in a loop through my drug-addled brain.

Maja had woken up when I grabbed the wheel out of her hands. She was stunned at the close-up sight of the red rock cliff, directly in front of her, and immediately grasped what had nearly happened. Leaping out of her seat, and despite having nodded off herself—admittedly, a much less serious offense than the captain of the boat doing so—she was angry and defiant, screaming at me, "You said to drive to the boat to Red Hill. I never drove a boat before. What the fuck! You almost killed us. You almost killed me! You got yourself blotto, Mr. Captain Mushroom Asshole."

This went on for several minutes. She stumbled around on the deck, lambasting me and glaring over her shoulder at the red rock wall the boat had almost hit. The commotion woke the others and her brother told Maja to shut up, he had a terrible headache. Tim, who had fallen out of the second fighting chair and hit his head on the deck when the boat abruptly changed direction, sat cross-legged holding his head. Casey and Sally, falling off the fish box, had grabbed each other's legs. They were in a jovial, carousing mood as they rolled on the deck untangling themselves.

Sally, oblivious to the near-death event, pulled herself together enough to stand up and put her arm around Maja's shoulder. All Sally saw was a woman in distress. She was clueless as to Maja's anger, fear, and confusion. But Maja shook Sally off; she was having none of it: the man she trusted and I hoped had fallen for was just another drugged-out bum. She crossed her arms and never looked at me once on the trip back to the harbor.

I headed toward the Keauhou Bay boat dock without talking to anyone. Waves of guilt and shame overcame me. My whole body shook several times. And then there was the vision that had been my salvation: how to process having a visitation from Quan Yin at just that moment, hearing—hallucinating?—her voice in the form of a clarion call for emergency action disguised in what I took as a romantic gesture.

The image kept coming back to me: my boat being lifted over the ragged boulders, the heart-stopping *thunk* and shudder as the rudder hit a mass of rock. I could not believe I had been enough of a swaggering idiot to eat all those magic mushrooms just to impress some drunken meth head tourists. And to turn the piloting of my boat over to a teenager with no experience, a teenager who herself was half-looped on mushrooms and weed. Also, it hit me that I did not have any approved life preservers on board, just floating seat cushions. Another sharp move, Captain Bud! If the boat had hit the rocks, gotten punctured and slipped back off the rocks, we would have been in deep water in a flash. I had no idea if any of my passengers could swim when sober, let alone intoxicated.

Overcome with belly-churning guilt, I wallowed in my larger than life shit show of failures. The nightmare averted kept getting worse in my mind, which was racing. There would have been an insurance claim. The Coast Guard would have investigated. No skipper license, no livelihood. Charges, probably felonies. My prospects of returning to academia dimmed to zero.

When I docked the boat, they all stumbled a bit and left. Bolt and his gang had had an adventure, and were in a light-hearted mood, off to drink more and take more drugs, probably. I watched Maja leave. She did not look back. I loaded the five bright-white *ono* into my truck and delivered them to the icehouse and went straight home.

The One That Got Away

Two days later I met Maja at the beach house. Her family was out trying to score big with some locals in the little town of Captain Cook, the focal point for growers of, notably, Kona coffee and Kona Gold. She was more beautiful than ever and our intertwining heartstrings were powerful. We agreed that we were done, but somehow, finally, ended up making intense love anyway. Talk only got in the way. She could not forget that I had almost killed her and her whole family by my stoner behavior. She would go back to Alaska with her brother. Leaving, I framed it all as another Hawaii vacation romance. But emotionally I was devastated. She lingered in my mind day and night.

Then a week later I saw her enter Bill's house. Bill was a friend and a gateway to my eventual spiritual awakening. We took some meditation classes together and occasionally talked about books, yoga, and the meaning of the concept of God. He also rented rooms month to month. I dropped by to say hello to him and of course to see Maja—if nothing else just to say hi.

One thing led to another and the flames soared as we leaned into them. It was still the dark of winter in Alaska and she told me that what she really wanted was a break from the crazies in her family. Suddenly my life revolved around her again. A week later she agreed to move in with me.

Unfortunately, my Red Hill warning did not wake me up to the reality of my spiral downward on multiple levels, spiritual, moral, and financial. I was in deep denial and still got stoned morning to night and drank all day.

Compared to my own drinking and smoking behavior, Maja's was moderate. She drove my pickup around town prudently and helped me a lot with the chaos of my life. Maybe she had always been an enabler like her mother, who had similarly enabled her alcoholic dad.

Inevitably, Maja left me. On a brief trip to San Diego to see my mom and dad around Christmas time I had recreational sex with several women. When I got back, Maja asked if I had been "good." After thinking about lying to her, or being completely honest for half a second, I nonchalantly told her I had only been with two women. At that time in my life, not lying and coming straight back to her was my idea of being a good boyfriend, especially factoring in the holiday season. What an idiot!

She was absolutely crushed. (Looking back, how obvious it was! What was I thinking? Was I thinking at all?) It was over! Over the next few days we hit rock bottom as a couple. She said she could not look at me without wanting to claw my eyes out. I was genuinely concerned and occasionally afraid when she chopped vegetables with the big kitchen knife while looking at me with hatred. The way she said it, so softly, was how you might expect a reserved but traumatized Scandinavian would speak, sort of matter-of-fact, flat-toned, with disgust in her eyes and a potential murder weapon in her hand. I deserved her hatred, anger, and contempt.

Our affair had lasted two months. When Maja said she was going back to Alaska, such was my deep depression that I did not fight to keep her, or even take her out for a farewell dinner. I could hardly talk to her or anyone else. I had been crushed—by me, myself, and I, my dream of true love and lust rolled into one destroyed life plan, down to a murky afterthought.

It's plain to see now that her leaving was for the best. Yes, she was the right age for starting a family. But the age difference. Would the kids have looked at me as a grandpa? Would the educational difference become a strain? Could I even support a family with my fishing and shabby lifestyle? I rationalized that I was unworthy of her: she had a productive lifetime ahead of her, and I was all too obviously a dead end.

In Maja's absence, the bills continued to pile up and boat issues drove me crazy. In full-bore denial, I reverted to type,: smoke a little more pot, play my guitar, plan for my next fishing trip, take the body of whatever woman put out the right signals.

But there were glimmers that the old ways no longer served me, that my emotional rollercoaster had turned into a tailspin. One evening shortly after Maja left, in bed I cried for the first time in my adult life. In a half-drunk stupor, I got up and walked, lunged, out of the house and stumbled around in the dark. Sobbing, I wandered into thick thorny, jungle-like brush near my house. When I got back inside, I was covered with small scratches from brush cuts, and my bare feet were cut by *a'a* lava rock.

Over the following weeks I spent a lot of time thinking. I sat for hours locked in cascades of remorse. What an asshole. What a stupid, drug-and alcohol-addicted blind man I had become. Strung out on the adrenaline rush of catching huge fish, taking local drugs, guzzling alcohol, and having easy sex. I was wasting my life. Was there something in my genetic makeup that had led to this dismal pass?

There were anguished moments of intense sweaty recall. Once, I lost three days to sleep. Other times I was overcome with gratitude for my vision of Quan Yin, which came back over and over. Why had it come at that moment, when I was blasted out of my mind, causing me to suddenly take action and save my passengers and myself? Was it a small change in the sound coming onto the boat as diesel engine noise reflected off the cliff? Did the smell of land, some waft of air carrying dust, trigger my survival response? Was it some kind of a psychic experience that made me aware of unseen force fields of energy?

I began to wonder if there were spiritual forces that carved out special life trajectories and key events. And whether all my activities had actually been laid out by God or spiritual beings before I was even born. Was *I* a spiritual being? Crazy thoughts, especially for a scientist by upbringing and twelve years of academic training.

These were the thoughts of a very mixed up guy threading together concepts my cousin Larry had introduced me to years earlier with a light touch. Books by and about Ram Dass, Idris Shaw, Rumi, and ibn el Arabi had intrigued me, maybe laying out the foundation for subconscious parameter changes.

Gradually it began to seem that I was floating on a cloud of redemption. If I was being saved for some higher purpose, it was best to be grateful. One afternoon I drifted into a spell of all-consuming love and gratitude for everyone and everything that had happened.

Redemption, however, would have to come after I faced the fact that my routine included at least one or two six-packs and getting stoned from before sunrise to late in the evening. Substance abuser was not a term in circulation back then but it applied to me. I was a walking, talking, functioning mess—like much of the rest of the fleet—my life filled with music, pretty women, beer, and an assortment of drugs to keep me awake for night fishing, or for running a charter and night fishing in the same twenty-four hours.

Even in my fog, I knew that somehow I needed to start paying attention to the big picture, to get up off my knees. And the world, my world, was changing. The *Pisces*, never particularly lucrative, had become a major liability, painfully expensive to keep running. It was becoming increasingly harder to ignore that I was rapidly going broke.

Disturbing lapses of ethical behavior come back to me from this period, the final act of my Kona fishing days. I still cringe at outright lies I told to good people. Once, offered a bribe, I easily accepted it, using the money to buy pot.

Such ethical lapses, as well as physical limitations, were becoming more and more obvious. On one long trip my legs gave out from exhaustion; my whole body hurt and shook. The grace period of eternal youth was giving way to early middle age. At some level, I was looking for an excuse to get out of the rut I was in. Flickers came to me, visualizations of myself as a family man instead of the guy at the hotel bar going home with yet another one-night stand. These flickers were the white flag I was starting to run up the mast. Surrender to adulthood! Was that even a possibility for me?

Then came the day when I told a charter to let a huge, beautiful blue marlin go. He nodded his head. Good! I wanted her to escape. She was magnificent and fought like hell. I said a small prayer for her and wished her well. I momentarily loved that glorious animal.

Rooting for that marlin to escape and win was the beginning of the end of my tenure as a charter boat skipper. I could no longer accept money to take people fishing. My heart was not in it. I did not want to club stunningly beautiful big fish to death anymore. I had to climb out of my deep, deep hole but did not really know how. What I did know was that something had to change.

10.
METAMORPHOSES

"The next step in man's evolution will be the survival of the wisest."
— DEEPAK CHOPRA

"**G**et married and have a family!" Enunciated loud and clear, the words sounded like they came through a megaphone. Whether the voice came from inside, on high, or was a hallucination or some kind of channeled communication, one thing was for sure: it was real enough to bolt me upright from my relaxed prone position. Looking around, I saw that there was no one else in the huge hall.

Before I reveal what called forth such an unambiguous commandment, I should say that on New Year's Day of 1979, Captain Bud, Phud (a play on the phonetics of PhD) went cold turkey. No beer, no wine, no pot. My friends in the fleet scoffed.

I didn't blame them. They only knew me as a pot smoking, bed hopping, Budweiser guzzling party animal. But that was before I met my future wife, then saw a poster at the health food store advertising a Sufi retreat on Maui, and the seeds planted by my cousin Larry began to take root. I did not have the money to fly to Maui and attend the retreat, which coincided with the full moon, but that very night, fishing in the near total darkness of a new moon, we got into a school of tuna and filled the fish box and covered the deck with valuable fish. It was a $10K night. Just like that I had the money to pay my debts and go!

The American Sufi movement was not identical to the strict Middle Eastern teachings and practices. Maybe they were akin to pizza in the States compared to the Neapolitan original. Many of the leaders were Jewish by origin. Some were cut from the cloth of the American Masonic and Rosicrucian movements, as in a code word, *rose*, whispered in my ear.

At the retreat, we did circle dances to the point of ecstatic experiences, but other activities were more on the order of kumbaya campfire music of love and sharing, roughly equivalent to early American Shaker dances that somatically imbue ethical values. We meditated, chanted, and interviewed the leaders, who mostly wore long, Egyptian-style robes. We slept in cabins on beds with army blankets and eat vegetarian meals in a large room. There was a lot of pot smoking by some leaders and none at all by others. One leader spoke of not wanting to be stoned and miss the invitation to the wedding party, referring to a New Testament parable.

There was a lot of sex in some of the cabins and family orientation in others. Potbellied trolls pursued young women around camp. Sincere yoga and tai chi types found their own corners. Long recitations of the Mahabharata forced their way into some of the proceedings and evening events. On the whole, a big, Hawaiian-style party with some serious inner work if you wanted it. I wanted it.

On the final afternoon, when most people had left, I stretched out on the hardwood floor of the spacious meeting hall. That morning, we'd all been doing Sufi dancing and Kundalini chanting since before dawn, culminating in an exercise in walking meditation. We were to imagine ourselves as spiritual leaders. I was assigned to be Moses, which felt somewhere between make-believe and the internalization of actually being enlightened. Pacing circles around the hall, I had pictured myself wielding a tall stick worthy of the Old Testament figure who received the Ten Commandments and led the Jews out of slavery in Egypt. (Others had been assigned to channel Jesus, Gandhi, or the Buddha.)

After everyone else had left, I lay stretched out flat on the hardwood floor, meditating and formulating a question: "What now, God?"

Though mostly I considered the answer—"Get married and have a family!"—an aftereffect of way too much immersion in Sufi rituals, its intensity was impossible to ignore.

❑ ❐ ❑

At the time there were no suitable women in my life. (Though that was about to change.) I still had a charter boat captain's lifestyle. I was unencumbered, still fooling around with vacationing ladies, mixed in with some lingering relations with locals. And marriage was not even remotely on my mind after the debacle of my whirlwind romance with Maja. I had pretty much resigned myself to the life of a philandering pothead, a forever-broke fisherman.

After the retreat ended, one of my roommates left, so I posted a rental notice at the local food coop, and a Coast *haole* woman wearing a mainland, mid-calf type dress answered the ad. Her name was Cynthia, and she needed a place for a few months. We gradually developed a friendship. Then she changed her plans, staying on and getting a job. When she told me she was moving out to go traveling with a girlfriend, it hit me that I did not want her to go. I even found myself imagining having a family with her, an unexpected feeling for me.

So I invited Cynthia out to fish on the *Pisces*, and up in the tuna tower, five miles offshore on placid blue water, spontaneously proposed. She was clearly surprised, even shocked.

When she looked over her shoulder, I wondered if she was considering how long a swim it would be to shore!

To make matters more unusual, before the proposal we had not had a romantic relationship at all, much less a sexual one. Being me, of course I had made my obligatory move, but after she declined I thought no more about it. Sure, we had watched breathtaking Kona sunsets together, though mostly with others around. And due to our domestic proximity there were few secrets between us; she had seen a number of women come and go over the preceding months.

Cynthia reacted to my brash proposal in a practical and matter-of-fact manner. We talked about it, then talked some more, then reached a consensus. The basic agreement was that she would move in with me that night—switching bedrooms in the house—and if we got along well for a year, we would get married. She emphasized that sex with another woman was a deal-breaker. I asked for a dispensation of one other woman a year. She said no. Her no was absolute! I knew when I was licked and agreed. Maybe that was the discipline I unconsciously wanted, and subliminally I was seeking boundaries.

She was not at all interested in my involvement with the Hawaiian Sufis, and when I wanted to go on one more retreat, she dropped me off at the Sufi Camp and went to hang with a girlfriend in Honolulu. The camp was at a Boy Scout retreat in the mountains on Maui. I arrived early and picked a cabin near the community toilet and meal room. Over the course of the day, four women moved in with me. It was a bit strange, yet by brief greetings and small talk it seemed fine. The cabin had four beds and a mattress on the floor, with little space to spare.

My cabin mates picked their spots. A thirty-something nurse with an eccentric personality took the bed next to me. The corpulent, Hispanic camp cook slept half-naked on the mattress on my other side. Two attractive young women took the other beds. Just into their twenties, they arrived in long white gowns and seemed like out-for-a-good-time college freshmen. The women lounged around topless in the cabin, maybe just relaxing, maybe to entice me into a typical Sufi camp sensual massage party. One played a reed flute and rolled her eyes at me, with the flute pushed down between her firm breasts. I was tempted but at the same time fully cognizant of my commitment to Cynthia. I smiled, nodded, and marveled at the draw of youthful feminine beauty, but was determined. When the thirty-something nurse bluntly propositioned me outright on the second day of the retreat, I said no, I was engaged.

Not that I was internally referencing what had happened with Maja; more like, this is a test! Pass-fail. No in-between score. In my meditations I noted the pull of lust, observing that pull in flashes of salacious mental imagery and organic, visceral, surging pulses of hormonal lust. But in the end, I knew then and there that I was ready to become a committed family man.

When Cynthia picked me up at the end of the third day and asked if I still wanted to get married, I asked her the same. Yes, we agreed. This was the beginning of my first sustained culturally dictated metamorphosis. My drives for risk through sexually casual relations, did not simply evaporate, although they were mitigated. They were akin to genies in a glass jar on a shelf visible to me and to her. With the lid on my id screwed on tight.

Almost exactly a year after I had proposed, a Hawaiian Kahuna priest officiated at our marriage ceremony. Cynthia and I had a terrific wedding. A total blast! Our parents paid to rent a big hotel garden for the venue. A friend brought his professional band to play dance music. Another went night fishing and caught a yellowfin just to contribute fresh sashimi for the party. The guests came from different ends of my business world: real estate and the charter boats. My Sufi friends brought a belly dancing troupe that I drummed with now and then. They shimmied and balanced swords on their heads. Even as we danced and my bride pushed cake in my mouth, we knew it was going to be a tough ride.

Cynthia and I spent a one-day honeymoon in a rough hewn, public park log cabin high on the chilly slopes of Mauna Kea, a dormant volcano, and started marriage counseling the next week! The complications leading up to our counseling are not germane here. Only let it be said that we both knew the huge, risky jump we were making, and some days we both shuddered and considered our union probably a big mistake. Still, we had come to a mutual decision, for better or worse, and we were going to give it a go.

In a short period, I had gone cold turkey on drugs and alcohol, made the first steps on the road to a spiritual path, and found a mate. Somehow I pulled out of my tailspin in the nick of time, a recurring happenstance with me. Yes, my appetite for risk draws me to danger like a moth to a flame, but I seem to shift course before meeting my doom.

When a small bomb went off in my hands and shrapnel gashed my lip, I stopped making explosives. The Mae West malfunction on my seventeenth jump was my final skydive. I got out of Africa instead of taking a new assignment elsewhere on the continent. And as much as I love scuba diving, after almost leaving this earthly plane underwater in Guatemala, I did not dive again for nearly twenty years.

In each instance I did a reset.

Or is there a DNA sequences that told me, "You are forty now, time to build a nest"? Perhaps a spiritual presence dictated that I had more work to do, work that required a home and hearth. Or it could have been as simple as common sense, gushing to the fore in my brain with the wisdom of humility, shouting in my ear, "You had it all and squandered it like a drunk on a binge. There is a better path. Savor the taste of other parts of the cornucopia of life, feed a different appetite." Such a major metamorphosis did not occur overnight, although it did prove relatively definitive.

Next, I had to figure out what to do about the *Pisces*, so I could start off married life with a clean slate. Times were tough. The catch rate plummeted as foreign long line boats, with strings of hooks and nets over a hundred miles in length, set their gear close to the Hawaiian Islands, taking all the tuna, marlin, swordfish, and sharks that were to be had. Bottom line, Captain Bud could not pay the bills.

Plus there were more mechanical problems with the boat, coinciding with my lack of funds. This was during the Carter presidency, when interest rates climbed to 18 percent to stem post-Vietnam inflation. In short, the global economy came to a crushing slowdown. People were not traveling to Hawaii for their vacations and no one wanted to buy Hawaiian real estate, though I did sell two vacant lots in those months, a home and condo. The commissions, however, did not amount to much.

Once, Cynthia and I even picked up a little pin money as extras for a Hollywood feature starring the English actress Jacqueline Bisset and Paul Newman. It was a terrible movie but we had a ball. I got a huge crush on Jacqueline and Cynthia had a flirt scene with Paul. It all seems rather silly in retrospect, though it gave us a chance to work together as a team. Making the most of my time on the set, I sort of bulldozed us into the extras community. I remember being flattered when Cynthia told me that a member of the casting team told her I was a beautiful man. I guess I was at the time, and yes, I have used my natural attributes to help get what I wanted more than once.

My looks, however, did not stop me from being ground down by my own issues and megatrends beyond my control. With my back to the wall, a sense of desperation and the need for a radical change crawled through my brain and my conversations with Cynthia.

All the while, as my attitudes and goals were changing, thanks to Cynthia's positive influence, my dockside life as a fisherman was getting increasingly uncomfortable. Twice, I was challenged to "Duke it out," right there at the docks. Both times I passed, ignoring the taunts as best I could. But violence was a surging undercurrent. A fellow fisherman was killed by a hard-faced woman I knew when he opened the door early one morning. Another died when he fell out of his Jeep in an opioid stupor. There was a gunfight between rival gangs at the dock where I moored my boat. I had to cross a yellow crime-scene tape and had my boat searched for drugs and bullets. There was also a mysterious man overboard event—he was killed by a shark.

One event around this time that I am proud of is stepping between two mismatched antagonists, a massive Hawaiian guy and a small, thin *haole* who was sarcastic and rude, someone there was not much to like about. But the Hawaiian was slapping him around at will, and the white guy was at serious risk of being knocked off balance and falling backwards onto a hard, flesh-lacerating volcanic rock ledge. He was on the verge of serious injury, or worse. When I stepped between them, facing the attacker, his blows landed on my shoulders and upper arm. I spoke in a soft, low voice, telling the Hawaiian, "Enough." I then stepped aside, and we all continued drinking our afternoon beer and talking about fish. In key ways this was a manifestation of my lifelong commitment to peace—and a reminder that I needed to get away from this environment.

The internal driver for radical change came through my

resolution to do the Sufi Burden Rock Ceremony. In simplest terms, the Burden Rock Ceremony is an internal process where you ascribe an issue to a rock. The rock becomes the symbol for a burden in your life. You can even write the name of the problem on the rock with chalk, or make a note and attach the note to the rock. Essentially, you must carry the rock a distance, uphill, so that your mind is forced to be focused on the single discomforting topic. (This type of moving meditation parallels similar practices by shamans and AA type organizations all around the world.)

Alone, I went to the base of a volcanic cinder cone just north of the Kailua-Kona small boat harbor, where I simply told myself that I had a financial problem and did not know what to do. Then I picked up a piece of pahoehoe, a kind of lava that weighed about two pounds and walked up the cinder cone hill. Twenty minutes later I reached the top and dropped the rock. I did not have an answer but sure felt glad to get rid of that jagged rock.

I did it again a week later, and this time my problem was clearly revealed. It was my boat, which was also my office, my independence, my main source of income, my pride and joy tool for doing what I loved most, fishing. It was clearer with every step up that hill. The time had come to divest myself of the *Pisces*. I advertised and sold it quickly to a real estate developer. According to rumors, sometime later he intentionally sank it at South Point for the insurance money.

Fortuitously, a nudge in a new direction came along at just the right time, in the form of a short part-time job on the MINI OTEC (Ocean Temperature Energy Conversion) barge anchored just offshore of the Kailua-Kona airport. The project was an early stage of truly innovative research; its results contributed to the electricity power mix of wind, solar, and conventional petrol-driven generators now routinely used in Hawaii. Our work concentrated on the temperature difference between deep cold water and warm surface water to phase-shift ammonia from a liquid to a gas to drive a turbine. Arcane stuff to the layman, but the goal was all-important: the generation of electricity. And it worked. I only served as a deckhand, but it was exciting to be part of a groundbreaking science project. Plus, the experience proved to be my first step toward honoring my wonderful education and engaging marine biology as a profession.

The next step was a change of scenery. Yes, there were risks involved, but I was determined to be a husband—and a father. Cynthia and I relocated to Honolulu, where I was able to put my advanced degree to use in the specialized universe of international marine biological consulting, taking long-term jobs in Oman and Burma (now Myanmar).[4] Cynthia traveled with me on both assignments, during which we were working hard to conceive a child, with no luck. Children did not come biologically but the spiritual journey was intensified. The intent to acknowledge and honor boundaries and internal, belief-based filters was leaking into my consciousness.

In Burma we spent important time with Theravada monks and nuns. Watching a young nun who mindfully sat down in slow motion, and a monk who had been cross-legged for an hour, come to full standing over a matter of minutes, while internally acknowledging each muscle and joint movement, left a profound impression on this observer.

What had brought me to Burma was a subcontract with the Asian Development Bank. I was tasked with assessing both the giant freshwater prawn (*Macrobrachium rosenbergii*) and the resources available to the Burmese government to pay back in hard currency a loan to upgrade processing and canning

---

[4] It was in Burma that the CIA offered to pay my rent in exchange for allowing them to use my house to interview Russian counterspies. No sale. Another time a slick but informally dressed man at an impromptu dinner party tried to recruit me. My critique of the Agency's abysmal track record caused him to freshen his drink and not return.

infrastructure. This work had me visiting random sampling blocks in the Irrawaddy Delta to determine both the catch per unit effort from different types of prawn fishing gear and how the local fishermen and women marketed their prawn catch. Technical stuff, as much of marine biology is in practice.

It was also risky, since Shan rebels operated in the Irrawaddy Delta, and Burmese gangsters and smugglers frequented the meandering channels of the Delta to move products in and out of Thailand. Naturally, I did not consider the risks, only that this was the scientific way to obtain real catch rate numbers. In big wooden Thai fishing boats captured from illegal operators, I made trips down the river channels with a whole retinue of Burmese political operatives and at least six fully armed soldiers.

Life on the boat was like rough camping and we ate local food only. I watched artisanal fishing practices and made notes on catch rates and local markets. Fascinating work (to me), although on one site visit I caught a bad case of hepatitis and passed out in a drainage channel, necessitating a two-day journey back to Rangoon to see a doctor. It turned out that I had non-A, non-B, non-C hepatitis. My liver was like a small watermelon. It took nearly six weeks for me to recover enough to continue my work.

During this period I learned a spiritual lesson based on a psychic healing for a disfiguring skin disease called "spider bite." The American Embassy doctor had no treatment to offer, while local people told me that if the skin problem circled my body I would die. A well-known local shaman, a middle-aged woman called Aunty Gyi, did a brief healing ceremony, demanding that I not watch her healing practice. I complied.

Over the next few days, the noxious, oozing skin condition was completely healed. A year later, back in Burma to continue the prawn research project, I went to Aunty Gyi to learn what she had done. She showed me and translated her prayer. That afternoon, I watched Aunty Gyi conduct a healing of a schoolgirl. Her daughter, a Western-trained medical doctor, told me her mom did this healing routinely and that she had no explanation. Aunty Gyi had been trained by her father. She was the only one in the family who could do it.

My encounter with Aunty Gyi illustrates a regular occurrence in my life: getting a terrible disease and recovering, or being saved in a life-threatening situation through circumstances beyond conventional understanding. Why was I always being saved by some entity or other? A little Mayan boy in Guatemala, a driver in Nigeria, a mental image of Quan Yin in Hawaii, meaningless words saluting a Nigerian King. Do protective spirits actually go around day and night working crazy hours just to keep me alive?

Ultimately, to start a family, Cynthia and I tried reproductive clinics, which proved to be no help. So we decided to adopt; after all, the world produced a lot of children and we could be parents to children who needed a mom and dad. To my great joy, we were deemed eligible to adopt a boy we named Tom and a few years later a girl we named Michelle. Both were from the Chulalongkorn Red Cross Hospital in Bangkok, Thailand.

One of my last overseas assignments, undertaken when we already had the kids, was a four-month stint in Alexandria, Egypt, working on an environmental impact report funded by the United States Agency for International Development (USAID). While there, despite having a family I still chose risky options and spiritual adventures over the mundane. To get to work, I elected to walk across a six-lane roadway instead of taking the company van. I usually timed my crossing to coincide with Egyptians also doing so, dodging slow-moving oncoming car and trucks. I did not say "Allah Akbar" as the Egyptians did while crossing; I simply walked the rest of the way to the office. But I did stop crossing that wide roadway after I saw an Egyptian get hit and dragged by a truck.

In the evenings, I ventured out more than the other Americans, bowing to the restlessness that is forever in me. One night I met Ali, an Egyptian secret police officer. We played chess and eventually became friends. After curfew, we would smoke strong, scented, hookah tobacco in stylish Middle Eastern cafés, after which I was escorted back to the guesthouse with Ali beside me and two men following. I eventually saw his pistol, hidden by his sport coat and tucked into his belt. For me, we were just playing chess and enjoying tobacco. For them, maybe it was something to put into a report to their superiors.

Also, there was a terse meeting with a heavyset man with a thin mustache, a leader of the Egyptian Palestinian community. I'd been told that he operated several fast-food restaurants in Alexandria. He kept looking at me suspiciously with a cigarette in the corner of his mouth. This guy seemed like someone who would nonchalantly pull the fingernails off an American to extract useful information. I heard smuggling was his game. Mine was simply adventure.

My guess is that Ali and the tough Palestinian believed I was CIA, using the USAID project as a cover, *Smiley's People* stuff, when in fact I was just a mediocre chess player with a taste for something unique. (Having been asked enough times, I guess I must look the CIA type.) After returning to the US, I got a postcard from Ali, my chess playing secret policeman buddy. Cryptically, it read: "KP to E4. Your move." I ghosted him. My interest in chess had waned and I did not consider it wise to continue a fraudulent relationship that might adversely affect my family.

❏ ❐ ❏

Of greater lasting impact from my time in Egypt were forays into Coptic Christianity and the Egyptian Book of the Dead. One weekend I took the train from Alexandria to Cairo to see the Great Pyramid. The entrance is a long low tunnel from the base to the central sarcophagus chamber. While inside, after the other crawlers left, I squirmed into the massive sarcophagus and lay on my back, arms crossed over my chest, where I was immediately flooded with a kind of welcome home feeling, and with hieroglyphic visions, and especially Egyptian cat images. An all-consuming, uplifting intensity overtook me.

When a fresh group of visitors entered the chamber, there was an audible gasp as I rose up out of the sarcophagus. I stood leaning against a back wall until everyone left, then approached the sarcophagus, put my hands on the side, and began to chant "OM." Others emerged out of the darkness; they approached the sarcophagus too, placing their hands on the side and chanting. Our ad hoc group somehow struck up a kind of polyglot harmony. We stayed until an armed guard insisted we leave.

Outside, we chatted. We were a diverse group, among us a German apple farmer doing Hari Krishna chants and two Greeks chanting Eastern Orthodox prayers associated with the ascension of the Virgin Mary. Through this experience, I first became aware of the Coptic text on the teachings of James and the Gospel of Thomas, which confused and captivated me for years until I better understood the essence of the Bhagavad Gita. As we said our goodbyes outside the tomb, it turned out that none of us had anything to write with so we could stay in touch. But somehow, one of them tracked me down and reached out thirty years later!

My four months in Egypt alerted me to the significance of domestic responsibilities. If I wanted to be a family man in reality, not just as a goal, we would have to all live in the same house and share daily routines. This realization did not immediately dovetail with financial equilibrium, as I was phasing out my international consulting practice to launch an aquatic biological consulting practice from scratch in the San Francisco Bay Area.

Assignments came, but only some were financially rewarding. A few stand out, such as working with importers of cultured giant clams earmarked for pet aquariums, and assisting in transshipping disease-free Atlantic salmon eggs from Finland to Chile. Securing this work did, however, demonstrate that my innate opportunistic assertiveness and self-confidence were paying off, and after a few thin years I started winning consulting bids in Northern California from government agencies.

I cannot say I was very good at this kind of work, and I made a few notable blunders, but I persisted and became involved in mitigating the impacts of pile-driving in the aquatic environment. (I discovered that underwater shock waves from pile driving ruptured the internal organs of fish, killing thousands.) Native oyster habitat restoration and using underwater acoustic tracking of salmon to validate habitat restoration were other really interesting projects. And I even won a bronze award plaque from Caltrans.

Gradually, I came to understand my ongoing professional metamorphosis, from industrialized fishing at Del Monte Foods, to commercial fishing in Hawaii, to a range of overseas projects, all of it culminating in aquatic protection from underwater noise pollution and habitat restoration. Overall, marine biology proved to be an eventful career, although there were distractions, notably a period of compulsive obsessive video gaming during work hours, an intermittent, embarrassingly dysfunctional behavior that affected my job performance. My career came to a close when at seventy-three I decided it was time to let the young people win the jobs. Since then, I have continued to do local marine biological consulting and expert witness cases when the work interests me and pays well.

On the domestic front, through years of counseling, Cynthia and I continued to sort things out as individuals (we definitely had personal issues), a couple, and parents. Although there were accommodations, I cannot say there was a metamorphosis on this front other than an increase in our ability to shrug off the small stuff. We rose to the challenges of each other's personalities and the demands of making the nut to pay the mortgage and maintain a household. Basically, though, by the end of our marriage we were who we were at the beginning of it. She had her issues too, but her story is her own to tell, not for me.

Still, we managed to hang in there for years and in many respects had an emotionally rich life as a family. We raised our children in the context of Christianity and Theravada Buddhism, attending seasonal ceremonies from both spiritual paths. Cynthia and I studied the many forms of Buddhism, did a lot of Vipassana mindfulness meditations, and attended local Thai temple celebrations with the kids. I was also much drawn to the channeled information from Seth, Abraham, and Edgar Cayce, and became a Northern California Course in Miracles leader.

Over the years, my spiritual path has seen me practicing tai chi, yoga, and qigong for decades, and I am a certified yoga instructor. I still teach in a park near my apartment, intermixing the disciplines. (For a while I was part of the Prison Yoga Project at San Quentin State Prison, where even though the inmates in the classes had been vetted for good behavior, it was unnerving to go through the double steel doors and realize I was the only person in the room who had not murdered someone.)

As well, my curiosity has led me to absorb scientific studies on consciousness demonstrating that instead of the five senses, we can now discuss inputs to the brain from something more on the order of twelve senses! And we know that elephants make very low frequency sounds we cannot hear; bees see colors we can't see outside the laboratory; and dogs smell scents unknown to us. As for ourselves, we cannot see magnetism, only the effect of it on certain materials. We in fact experience very little of everything going on around us. We just do not have all the sensors needed to detect all of it, nor the brain processing power.

❏ ❐ ❏

During my marriage to Cynthia, it was not all serious spiritual practice, though. We also went to our children's sporting events, sang and read the kids to sleep, and went on vacations and political protests, plus spending time with our extended families. Golf and music were prominent family features. Both Tom and Michelle especially loved the game. We were probably a bit over the top in our collective competitive natures but it remains a pivotal family feature.

Cynthia and I made it work for thirty years and ended our marriage with a minimum of emotional and financial contortions. Recently, we have been able to high-five each other for a job well done, or at least jobs well done given who we were, warts and all.

The years following our separation and divorce saw me having several affairs and getting married again, very briefly. I often found myself looking at the man I was before I got married.

The Man–Woman Thing

A female friend who knows me well once said, "Once you lock eyes on an interesting woman, you become like a predator. You change from being a goofy younger brother to an animal." Ouch! But I think she's right. Something to be mindful of and work on in an era where romance and sex addiction are contro-versial topics. I also admit to getting some insight from partici-pating in some AA type sex and romance group meetings.

But I do not see myself as a total knuckle-dragging dick-head. Well, sometimes, but I am proud of my role in the life of Myrna, who was my lover and deckhand for a year in Hawaii. I encouraged her to get her skipper's license, and when she be-came the first female licensed charter boat skipper on the Kona Coast, I was damn proud and let her run my precious boat in tournaments and when I had a charter but wanted to go night fishing instead.

Since my split from Cynthia, I have had relationships lasting from the time it take to finish a cup of coffee to several years. Yet every breakup is still painful, emotion-rocking. Then come the depressions and hours beating myself up for playing the game of love so badly. Relationships blossom, evolve, and have their sunset moments. Yes, a few have ended badly, even with me threatening to call the police, and in one case doing so. But you do not go into therapy because of the rush of falling in love again and again. You go because of the pain of the fallout time after time. During the down times it is almost impossible to understand that endings lead to insight and how a door closed reveals other openings.

Overall, my interactions with women are more multifaceted now. Sex is no longer the main driver. In Kathryn, my colleague in a spiritual retreat enterprise, I have a dedicated business part-ner. That relationship has generated a profound explosion of creativity and joy. I have several other female business collabora-tors, including a Hispanic mega-mom and an African American lesbian. Through knowing them, I am richer far beyond good numbers on a financial balance sheet.

Harmonious interpersonal relationships of any kind re-quire mindfulness. In spite of my good score on a multiphasic personality test, I do not consider this an area where I excel without consistent effort. But it is likely that my warm acknowledgement of the people around me is reflected in the angels referred to earlier who have pulled my bonehead ass out of the fire over and over again.

Daring to Sing out Loud

Throughout my marriage to Cynthia and beyond, music has been a big part of my life. I have played the guitar and sung often with friends and family. Eventually, I performed at Davies Symphony Hall in San Francisco, and also at Carnegie Hall and on the Main Stage of the Country Music Hall of Fame in Nashville. Every one of these occasions was a bit of a fluke, like so much else in my life, but they were consistent with my nature to explore and take actions without fear. (At least no one ever threw a tomato!) I have a rich, deep, bass voice and can be enthusiastically loud. I have memorized the chords and lyrics to hundreds of songs and attempt to memorize a new song every few months.

Music will always be my main brain health tool. A soul-piercing jam is a great boon to relationships. In addition, playing music with others triggers neural receptor and cranial blood flow. It excites listening, timing, harmony, neuromuscular synchronization, memory draw, and vocalization—all at the same time. Imaging studies have documented that when musicians play together, their whole brains get a workout, a neural symphony of dendrite and ganglia dancing the night away! Just for fun, I perform with others whenever I can. Musicians are among my closest friends.

Risky Business

Structurally, I have been a producer-investor in diverse ventures, the money man who can financially make an idea come to fruition. In my fifties, an adventure full of gusto resulted in *The*

Bonefish Chronicles, a documentary centering on indigenous fishermen inhabiting Tarawa Lagoon, Kiribati. The project was set up by the USAID as a way to push money on a tiny Pacific island nation so they would vote in the UN the way our government wanted them to. When the agency wanted a documentary summarizing the making of an island nation fisheries management plan, I produced the film, raising the money through USAID, hiring professionals, and nurturing a remarkable product in both English and Micronesian. No fear of failure!

Other than my stock portfolio and a few real estate holdings, my investments are centered on startups, including solar technology, innovative construction technology, and a hyperbaric oxygen treatment chain. My CPA said multiple times, "Only invest as much as you are comfortable losing, since that is generally what happens." But I know I am essentially investing in people. Even if a startup fails, I know I was helping innovators trying to benefit our culture.

An Audacious Endeavor

Technical reports and proposals in the third-person-passive voice were part of my life in marine biology. Eventually, though, instead of writing about the catch per unit efforts of indigenous fishermen in Oman, I discovered the urge to tell stories. To not just report facts but connect the dots. I was entranced and wanted to chronicle the courage of young men who sailed out onto the Indian Ocean in canoes made of palm fronds that had to be dried for several days before they could be used again. I was sure the burka-clad women who split and salted tuna at the beach had a story. I saw big fish draped across the backs of donkeys being driven inland by young boys, to huge mud-brick cities in the coastal highlands. I walked past clusters of armed men with ancient rifles that reportedly only limited banditry and rape.

In short, I hungered to write narratives about the people who intersected with my peripatetic career. One that I particularly hope to get around to is the Pickleweed Point Oyster Debacle.

Writing did become part of my life, gradually, with the goal of reaching a general audience. One completed project is *TRANSFORMATION*, a slim but potent nontechnical book of tai chi movements, affirmations, and commentary, issued in 2021 under the Peace Corps imprint. My friend and co-author Zochi Young inspired me in an inner journey on the somatic effects of linking tai chi movements to valuable interpersonal skills. Zochi is a true master of tai chi and Zen meditation. He and I come from far different backgrounds but share hope for humanity. I am a white guy from a beach town with a save-the-world attitude and he is an African American from Detroit with many wellness projects underway in the continental US and several East African countries.

I even tried to write a novel, set in Hawaii, but shelved it in favor of this memoir. Sweating it out to get my story right has been gut-wrenching at times. But the appetite for risk seems to have pushed me on to speak my truth, through countless drafts.

One saving voice has been my always-quotable brother, Greg: "These events took place fifty or sixty years ago and you have the audacity to think you can remember this stuff? You can't even remember phone numbers or birthdays or the name of the guy you met ten minutes ago."

My response: "But phone numbers and birthdays didn't try to kill me! You cannot unremember near-death experiences. You can only put it on a shelf. I will put it back on the shelf when I finish the damn book!"

❏ ❐ ❏

I increasingly see myself as part of the biome of Earth, someone with a genetic predisposition for curiosity, adventure, and sex. We humans are a variant species offshoot of the bonobo chimpanzee, with the ability to do things like drive a car. Just another life form temporarily populating the planet. From that perspective, good or bad, right or wrong are a bit meaningless. And shifting my perspective to acknowledging non-dual reality has become easier through my spiritual readings and practices. Everyone might not agree but it does make for clear thinking and peace of mind.

11.
TOUGH SEEDS

"No one can be free who has a thousand ancestors."
— EMILY CLIMBS

Our family history is pretty clear back at least ten generations, according to my brother Greg and sister Susanna, with some branches coming over from England in the early 1700s. These ancestors were serious. Weeks of suffering on wooden sailing vessels in the pounding Atlantic swells was not for the risk-averse. Their offspring married into other immigrant families and kept moving across the continent ("Go West!"); landowners and a few doctors, lawyers, businessmen, and architects emerged out of the gene pool. One great grandfather operated a roadhouse. Another had a theater in frontier Idaho.

Generational stories find echoes in my early childhood, hinting at an ancestral set of behavioral genes that expressed themselves throughout my life. In any case, family tales galore have helped me trace my roots as an entertainer, scientist, entrepreneur, and serial risk-taker. As kids, we heard Mom's stories innumerable times, told with a chuckle and a glass of white wine in hand. In the late 1920s, the young Mildred climbed Mt. Rainier without anything resembling modern gear for protection from the elements (in fact, she carried the injured guide down a glacier to safety). And on the Inca Trail in Peru, she hung from the roots of a tree over a thousand-foot cliff until the guide came back and rescued her. By then she was in her seventies. In her eighties she injured her foot climbing into a Canadian helicopter to escape a charging polar bear! My own behaviors and faith in survival are no doubt linked to the "can you top this" nature of family dynamics. Thanks, Mom!

Mom's father, Bob, told us stories too. He spent a lot of his early life in lumber camps across North America. There, he encountered Native Americans regularly. On camping trips in the mountains, he would show us how to read animal tracks and demonstrated Native American sign language. We were spellbound, but I now know it was also a key in opening me up to alternative communication modalities. Dad was a gateway too, into other languages: he spoke Spanish during camping trips to Mexico and sang German songs at Christmas. Over the years as I traveled and worked all over the world, I spent a lot of energy learning, if not mastering, Spanish, French, Yoruba, Itsekiri, Arabic, Burmese, Micronesian, and Hawaiian. I was FS-1 (Foreign Service) in all these tongues at one time or another.

Of endless fascination to me and my siblings was that Grandpa Bob had been a "powderman." He was not big, but the way he was built, solid and strong with a low center of gravity, opened up a career for him. He could walk and ride the massive logs floating downstream. In his day, lumberjacks cut huge trees in the summer months and oxen would pull the logs down to the edge of the rivers. Then the winter rains would swell the rivers, floating the logs. Bob's job was to give the floating logs a poke or pull with a long pike pole to set them in a linear direction and guide them downstream into the basins adjacent to the sawmills.

Sometimes there were massive logjams, dozens of logs piling up like a small mountain, leaving nothing to feed the sawmills. He would walk out onto them, rocked by turbulent moving rivers, and place dynamite between key logs, then stretch out the fuse line and set off an explosion to blow the logjam apart. Thus, his handle as a "powderman." Later he worked in the E.I. Dupont dynamite factory in Dupont, Washington.

My mom was born in Dupont. She recalls how the women in town would wait on their front porches for the men to return after the all too frequent factory explosions from TNT powder dust in the air. After a few factory explosions, Bob quit and bought a farm to focus on his young family.

Having heard these stories, of course Greg and I had to make our own dynamite. I purchased sulfur powder and saltpeter at the Ocean Beach pharmacy, on different days. We got lampblack from the local hardware store. Fuses for rocket-like toy airplanes were adapted to our purpose. We consulted *Encyclopedia Britannica* and spent weeks trying various mixtures to find something that burned fast. Once we nearly set the house on fire, after tossing some failed batches into a corner trash can that burned nearly to the ceiling of our underground factory.

But eventually we got the right mix and started blowing stuff up. One explosion sent a large piece of metal into our neighbor's lovely redwood fence. Our explosive-manufacturing careers came to an end when a small bomb blew up in my hands and sent a shard of plastic into my upper lip. Bleeding profusely, I ran to the bathroom and saw myself in the mirror. That was too much. Grandpa parted company from dynamite when it got risky, and we quit when I got hurt. Knowing when to quit dangerous stuff is also in my genetic makeup: a single Mae West malfunction midair was enough for me!

❑ ❐ ❑

On the other side of the family, my great-great-grandfather George's exploits in the US Mounted Rifles, Company C, stand out. He later settled in southern Idaho and raised a family. He missed direct participation in the Civil War due to near fatal injuries sustained in a train wreck. At the time he was an "Indian Agent" on his way to Washington, D.C., to report on treaties and business affairs on reservations. He later married the daughter of a prominent Quaker family in Perry County in southern Pennsylvania; she nursed him back to health. Perry County was a prominent link in the "Underground Railroad," spiriting slaves out of the South. There is no family record of his participation in that effort, but it seems likely.

Still in his early twenties, George Abbott was an Indian Agent for the federal government, forcing Native Americans onto reservations. His role in our genocide of them makes me cringe. His story is included here in the context of his appetite for risk and mine. I cannot defend US policy toward Native Americans, then or now.

One story George handed down *does* makes me proud, however, from after he left the military and served as a Captain of the Civilian Volunteers. It took place against the backdrop of lethal confrontations in northern California and southern Oregon, as families from the Midwest and East moved west after the Gold Rush. Along with three other vigilantes George was tracking a group of renegades who had murdered five men in the Ledford party, which was trying to cross the Cascades in the Klamath Lake area. He and his cohorts made camp around twilight, when they heard horses and were confronted by nine armed Native Americans; two of them he recognized as the renegades responsible for the Ledford party massacre. His companions leaned against trees with blankets over their legs, guns hidden, at the ready. All the while, George sat on a log, whittling with a large Bowie knife, and engaging them by talking about reservation business. This went on for hours.

The situation must have been extremely tense, everyone eyeing each other, wondering who would shoot first. I picture them in the darkness, in a forest, miles from any backup or help. The men under the blankets likely whispering among themselves, scared out of their wits, hands on their weapons. The renegades must also have been wary, conversing about the white men with obvious guns under their blankets, and which of them to shoot and in what order. Then there was George, sitting on a log, whittling! His backup plan: stab the man nearest him at the onset of hostilities.

According to George's account, he ultimately calmed everyone down by using words. He engaged in palaver in the local language, broken English, and the words he had learned in his years as an Indian Agent. After about four hours, the murderers and their renegade companions got on their horses and went back to the reservation. No one was killed. George had talked his way out of a potentially lethal battle. To reiterate, I know that there is much wrong in George's actions, but again, I am presenting it here unflinchingly to demonstrate his appetite for risk and verbal skills.

The above episode resonates with my own actions and reactions, notably in Hawaii with Pauly, the drunk felon who flashed a knife before brandishing a gun and pointing it at me; and also when I was accosted by river pirates in the Niger Delta with words my only weapons. All of this has led me to conclude that talking my way out of some deep caca must be part of my genetic makeup.

❏ ❐ ❏

In an old family photo album, my Great Aunt Bert stands beside her horse, her left hand on the bridle. Two whitetail bucks with big racks of horns are slung sideways. She carries a carbine rifle across one arm. The year must have been around 1910. Great Aunt Bert set a high bar. It was almost as if I, the oldest male, had to follow suit, as if it were imprinted on my mind, beliefs, and my DNA: I had to shoot a deer.

The opportunity arose when I was doing research for my grad school project. After getting my deer tag, I had been hunting without success throughout the fall. I tried a bow and arrow but only got off one shot. A clear miss. Later I tried stalking deer and waiting hours on a platform in the trees.

But on a clear afternoon I spotted a big white-tailed buck swimming across the lake where I was conducting my thesis research. As I sat down to eat, I saw the buck in a mirror of the field station cabin, and grabbed my shotgun from the brown and yellow gun bag, rapidly loading three 12-gauge slugs and slipping out the door to hide behind protruding cabin logs.

As the buck, with its impressive rack of antlers, stepped up on the bank of the lake, I sprung from my hiding place, leaping down through the lush fern and salal undergrowth. When I was some six feet away, the buck tried to get its back feet on ground to leap away. I shot it in the neck just behind the head. The shockwave of the marble-sized lead-metal slugs must have radiated up and down through the spine and scrambled the brain, killing it instantly. In fact, upon butchering the deer, it was easy to see that the slug had hit the spinal bone at the base of the skull. No thrashing and convulsing for this animal nearly as big as myself, slowly bleeding out. It was a clean kill. I was grateful for the animal's quick death, and paused to thank that big, beautiful, white-tailed buck for his life. A sort of respect thing I do even when I catch a fish.

Then I gutted and skinned it, and per the directions in the hunting guidebook I had carried with me everywhere for months, I hung the pink carcass up in the old brown tool shed for about a week to cure before properly butchering and sharing it with neighbors and research team colleagues. There were a few inches of snow on the ground at the time; it was the perfect temperature for the tenderizing effect of letting the meat tissue slowly break down. The result was lean meat with a hint of the forest. Maybe a subtle aftertaste of tannins from the plants that it had feasted on. While I no longer hunt game, I did for much of my life, starting early. I come from a long line of hunters and fishermen. Nor do I own a gun anymore, but guns—and knives—played a part in my younger life. The downside of guns is that it is easy to kill someone else or yourself. When I was about thirty and a graduate school research assistant at the University of Washington, I almost killed myself with a shotgun. I was going through a tough spell. (As a friend once said, "Life is like lumpy gravy. If you like gravy on your turkey dressing, sometimes you get a mouthful of lumps.")

I also still trout fish every year, but cut the barbs off the hooks. Sort of PETA fishing in streams and lakes.

❏ ❐ ❏

Knives were another part of my cultural inheritance. My brothers and I always had pocket knives. Every birthday we got a new one. We would carve planks into wooden pistols for our big shootouts, running around the house, dying dramatically or protesting loudly. "You missed," one of us would shout, as the other went "*RRRRRRR*," a tongue-rattling noise meant to sound like a machine gun. All great dopamine-rushing fun. The knife I used to butcher the white-tailed buck was virtually identical to the knife Pauly would later flash on me in Hawaii—although his sheath with leather tassels was orders of magnitude more impressive than my plastic knife sheath covered with a camouflage cloth pattern.

You know by now that I contend that the appetite for risky business—and to be specific, my own—has its roots partially in upbringing. Notably, there were the stories of Mom's derring-do in the Andes and our witnessing Dad's casual approach to smuggling goods in from Mexico on camping trips. More general behaviors also were fostered, such as our seeing Dad skin a dead raccoon, cure the skin in the sun, and sew it into a Daniel Boone raccoon hat. Watching him do so likely prepared me to skin a dead cow in Monserrat. Accompanying him and his friends on a rabbit drive almost certainly predisposed me to enter the hunting community at the University of Washington. My own behaviors and faith in survival are no doubt linked to a healthy dose of competition in our family dynamic.

Early on, Greg and I had learned how to pick mushrooms, and identifying the edible ones. Small round white mushrooms with pink gills were as close as the front lawn, back lawn, and adjacent vacant lot. Mom stirred them in with eggs. That experience likely propelled me to join the Seattle Mycological Society and later choose to eat chanterelle mushrooms instead of killing myself.

Camping trips with Mom and Dad taught me a lot too. I learned that any new endeavor was not guaranteed to be a success, and that like other predators we need to be persistent. Even the powerful, efficient big cats are only successful about a third the time. For a beginning deer hunter, one in seven is probably not bad.

❑ ❐ ❑

Greg and I killing each other was not a serious threat, but we did get in major fights, complete with gun threats. Yes, it is natural for brothers to fight; the Bible starts with a mesmerizing sibling murder story. Which I take as a cautionary tale, and thankfully so did Dad, who responded to our mutual threats by hiding our 22-caliber rifles. All in all, Mom and Dad's hands-on parenting allowed my continuity of gun-related experiences to unfold while maintaining personal safety and survival.

Hunting in general (not just deer) played a part in my development. The 12-gauge shotgun I purchased at the University Washington was a big deal. I hunted grouse and quail along the parameter of the Christmas tree farm near the field station. Knut, a mixed German shepherd lab, who came to Patti and me as a puppy, was a natural hunter. I trained him for bird hunting. After my quick read of a training manual and a few hours throwing things, plus reward kibbles, Knut could hold, watch where two things fell, and retrieve them sequentially. Great fun.

❑ ❐ ❑

When I was camping in the Kalalau Valley on the island of Kauai, I hunted feral goats. (Hawaii had—and has—a feral goat problem.) At the time, I was usually naked like everyone else there. My food was fast running out, and when I heard goats on a ridge above my camp site, I sprang into action, borrowing baling wire from a neighboring camper. I quickly set up three snares along the trails the goats used to gain altitude toward more grass and fewer trees. The next morning, we dashed up the trails, naked and shouting, and I got a big goat and a kid. I released the kid but butchered the adult and shared the meat with other naked campers in the valley. Some of them did not like it that I had killed a living animal. Most just laughed, cooked the meat over wood campfires, and ate well.

Butchering a dead cow in Montserrat as part of my Peace Corps training preceded my deer hunt, and that preceded my goat hunt. I can now see a continuity throughout my life, starting with ancestors who lived to the fullest. Their skills, actions, and survival mechanisms set the table for my own.

12.
RETURN TO
AFRICA

*"You cannot leave Africa. It is always with you,
there inside your head."*
— Bridget Dore

Having left Nigeria under fire fifty-one years earlier, vowing never to return to the continent, I was finally ready to replace the memories of my malaria-ravaged farewell at gunpoint with new images of exotic insects, colorful birds, and charismatic megafauna.

Almost eighty, I thought this might be my last chance. So I decided to go big. The hungry ghosts of desire swallowed up common sense and I joined a walking safari in South Africa organized by Biologists without Borders, a nonprofit committed to protecting our planet's progressively smaller populations of megafauna. Our mission would not involve killing anything, just tracking, catching, and tagging elephants, hyenas, and birds for research.

The group's leader and founder, biologist Sue Orloff, whom I have known for thirty years, raises funds for the preservation of African wildlife through projects that include supplying boots, night vision goggles for the anti-poaching teams, memory chips for trail cameras, and radio tracking collars. Sue is disarmingly charming, humble and knowledgeable and passionate; she looks at animals with loving concern for their well-being, and has been to southern Africa many times, while still relishing every bird call and predator track in the sand. The rush of a surprise sighting of antelope or Cape buffalo along the undulating edge of forested islands lights up her face.

Biologists without Borders also acquires large parcels of farmland to expand existing game reserves. Recently, they purchased enough farmland to connect two large, well-managed game reserves as a wildlife migratory corridor. Their next project is to build twelve-feet high electric fences in that corridor to help keep the wildlife in and farm animals out. Though electric fences will have an effect, to some African wildlife they are essentially just a strong suggestion. Impala and leopards can leap them in stride. A rutting bull elephant would likely not even notice the fence it crashed through to meet up with a female in estrus.

My travel arrangements to get to South Africa included a three-day layover in Dubai, where I had booked a room in the tallest hotel in the world, the Gevora, all of 77 floors, which resonated with my email handle, Bud Abbott 777. (Grandiosity can do strange things to the point of view.) The last time I had been in the UAE was 1972, when it was basically a mud hole with low cinderblock buildings, corrugated iron roofs, and a few wooden dhows lining the riverbank. Now, I would be landing in a magnificent modern metropolis, a fitting locale to process my feelings before returning to Africa.

Owing to the occasion, I flew business class, to allow myself to sleep and pamper my left leg, still on the mend from a recent body surfing incident. It hurt like hell! Surfing accidents happen all the time. No big deal. But the bruise was big and deep into the muscles. It hurt to walk. No matter. I had left Africa with health issues, so it seemed OK to return with them.

My first day in Dubai, I had an eight-thirty tee time at a golf and country club. A bit pricey but this was my one and only chance to play the course. The clubhouse was elegant, almost opulent, and the fairways a rich green from tons of dechlorinated sea water and a soil nutrient treatment impossible anywhere else. It was warm out; the humidity was low, the air was clear.

The next morning, I hit the driving range an hour earlier, and the golf cart manager gave me a set of slightly used Pings and a small ice chest with two bottles of water. Even this early, the temperature and humidity had shot up compared to the previous day, and a trickle of sweat rolled down my forehead as I practiced putting. I bogeyed the first two holes but on the third I parred, thanks to a pro-worthy shot out of a bunker to within in a yard of the pin. Overall, I was satisfied with my play: long straight drives and serviceable irons to the fringe of some very challenging undulating greens.

By the fifth hole the temperature was rising fast and I was chugging water and starting to fall apart. A blue face cloth had come with the cart. I wrapped it around a few ice cubes and placed it in my wide-brimmed safari hat to cool off my head. My next tee shot was wild, ending up in a sand trap at the base of a steep sinuous canyon. My second shot went into a lovely waterfall—a lost ball on the scorecard.

Climbing up out of the bunker proved challenging. Frustration clanged in my mind. My left leg still hurt and I slumped in the cart. The next hole was just 175 yards. I pulled out my black Ping hybrid. It flew out of my hands as I swung. I was shaking— in two hours the temperature had shot up to over 105.

Not my day. I was done. Overdone. Heat exhaustion. I bid my group goodbye and dashed for the air-conditioned clubhouse, where I poured water over my head and shirt. An hour passed before I could do anything more than sit.

Then I took a taxi back to the hotel. The taxis in Dubai are all Prius-type hybrids, station wagons with good air conditioning. The driver was friendly, chatting about going home for two months a year for the last ten years. His children were in good schools now. For my part, I talked about chilling the rest of the day. The joke was on me. Sleep in a cold air-conditioned room was the only thing on my mind. The golf heat stroke debacle had not helped my mood at all. On top of which, my left leg was still bothering me, a lot; a large blue and yellow bruise from hip to knee underscored the pain. I was very uncomfortable and more than a bit irritated.

In my hotel room, on the 48th floor, napping in the late afternoon with the TV on was easy. On CNN, an announcer detailed a Russian plane crash-and-burn, and a Cuban plane that had gone off the runway. In sports, Steph Curry, hero of my home team, the Golden State Warriors, missed an easy three pointer. Somehow a sense of the ominous was creeping into my jet-lagged brain. For some reason, for the first time in my life I regretted not buying travel insurance.

At about seven-thirty in the evening I was awoken by loud noises in the hall. Initially I took the source to be a wedding party, or some noisy Russian tourist. Then came a loud pounding on my door, which didn't stop. Opening the door, I and saw a big man in a black uniform pounding on the door next to mine. "What the fuck! I'm trying to sleep here," I shouted.

The big man turned to me and in a heavy Indian accent said, "Fire, sir, you must leave immediately." A smaller man with a yellow vest marked "Security" appeared and said, "Come now, Mister, you must run downstairs!" Swirling clouds of gray smoke wafting from the ceiling to the orange-and-gold-carpeted floor of the hallway had my total attention.

I knew I had to get dressed, thinking that they may find my

charred body but it will be clothed, not in my skivvies. It was one of those mad scramble moments you are never quite ready for. With the two men holding the door and alternatively shouting and pounding on other doors in the hallway, I pulled on my REI safari pants and sweat-soaked aloha golf shirt. Of course I was aware enough to grab the traveler's essentials: passport, wallet, and cellphone.

The big man reached into an abandoned room service cart and handed me a white face cloth and a small bottle of water. The water was for the face cloth. It seemed to help with blocking some of the smoke. With only black flip-flops on my feet, I was directed to the stairwell, which was dense with grey smoke. I started down the dimly lit, on-again off-again stairwell, holding the washcloth to my mouth and nose and keeping a hand on the rail in the dark sections. A few floors down I paused to pour more water onto the washcloth. My legs were starting to hurt. Each step down was a measured, cautious, painful effort in the semi-darkness.

As each flight took a toll on my thigh muscles, the magnitude of staying on the 48th floor dawned on me. My left leg—the one with the collision bruise—hurt the most. All the while, I heard screaming and crying above and below. A cacophony of pounding noises and shouts from the rescue team was disorienting. It was chaos. An Asian couple passed me chattering and coughing. A trio of young women speaking and shouting in an East European language pushed by me, almost careening down the steps.

I groaned, then crouched in a stairwell corner, said out loud to some imagined spiritual guide or angel, "I'm too old for this shit."

Halfway between floors I began to huddle in corners and let others pass. A glance through a window in a side door showed a cleaning staff supply cart turned on its side as if the crew had fled in haste. To one side, a bronze piece of furniture blocked an elevator door; a slab of decorative rock blocked another door. A big man with a West African accent was encouraging an African woman who was crying and screaming with leg pain to keep going. They had come down from the 60th floor. My challenge of coming down from the 48th floor paled in comparison.

The man had a large suitcase and little patience. He left the woman with me and charged down the stairs with his suitcase. I told her to breathe to get more oxygen. Just after this, two Eurasian men in hotel uniforms came up the stairwell, appearing out of the smoke like magic. They wore soft paper masks to cover their mouths and noses, and fumbled in their pockets, spilling masks on the steps. They handed some to the woman and me. One man gave me another bottle. They offered to try to carry the poor woman (she weighed more than their combined weight).

With one man under each of her shoulders, the crying woman was slowly helped down the stairs. I later learned that many of the hotel staff were from Nepal. The many flights of stairs were all in a normal day's trek for them.

By now my eyes were burning and I was coughing more. A man passed me, saying that if I could get to the 12th floor, everything would be OK. He was very encouraging: just twenty more floors to go. But my thigh muscles were screaming with lactic acid burn and my ankles were like painful nobs. Strangely, the flip-flops, though, were still intact. Out of the haze a man with a yellow vest appeared and waved at me to go to a side door. Somehow I had made it to the 12th floor! Here, the smoke was less prominent.

On the 12th floor, a causeway connected the hotel to the parking garage and swimming pool deck. Another man beckoned me forward to a service elevator filled with construction material. Out a window of the parking garage I could see the lights of fire rescue vehicles and ambulances flashing across the parking area at the foot of the building. With small painful, tentative steps, a white-haired old man, me, walked out of the elevator into a crowd of milling guests and hotel staff.

A group of men cleared a space for me to sit on a low wall. I was exhausted. Slack-jawed, head-dropped, eyes staring straight ahead, I sat on the wall still clutching my white facecloth and small bottle of water. Minutes passed and bit by bit I slowly came to myself. Fumbling hands confirmed I had my passport, wallet, and cellphone. Nearby, a young Arab woman in a white wedding gown sat on the ground surrounded by her female friends in black Arab gowns. Russian, Albanian, and Middle Eastern men and woman milled about, chattering in small groups. Hotel staff, cooks, room service, and doormen stood and watched, clustering by their employment status or ethnicity.

Bottles of water were offered to everyone. Several late-middle-aged English women in only white hotel bathrobes with swimsuits underneath gathered near a security tape. They had been at the pool when the fire broke out. They laughed and did little catwalk model displays with their white calf-length bathrobes. The big African woman I had encountered many floors above came over and sat down beside me. Her boyfriend joined, laughing. We had all made it OK. She was ecstatic to see the man who had abandoned her to save the big suitcase—but all was well. The suitcase had their passports. We all laughed together. He was OK. They were OK. I was OK.

A big bus took us to another hotel. I showered and then collapsed. My possessions on the 48th floor of the tallest hotel in the world and the trip to South Africa were past and future. The Now was all I could comprehend. Profoundly fatigued, I later managed to walk around gingerly on very sore legs, and near midnight managed to get a short email off to friends and family.

The next morning the sounds of the call to prayer, from a

prominent mosque across the street, woke me on my new 36th floor bedroom. It was not quite dawn, but there was just enough light for the chanters to see a thin black thread held at arm's length in the sky (traditionally the sign for prayers to commence). Just enough light in the sky to enable an old man who longed to be spiritually awake to resonate with the reminder that everything and every moment is sacred.

After yet another near-disaster, an awareness of the blessing of life seemed to assert itself. The need to do a gratefulness meditation swept over me. I took sixty long deep breaths, held at the top and the bottom of the cycle, long enough to feel the act of breathing and the flow of the Life Force's energy field pulsing through me.

"Thank you knees. Thank you ankles," I said. "Thank you black flip-flops. Thank you men who climbed up the stairs. Thank you Divine Presence." I thought of the Buddhist teaching about the fire that consumes lives with dissatisfaction. "Thank you Life Force that pushes me on." Reflections on an action-packed life: "If I will not or cannot walk into danger, the Life Force will dutifully bring it to me. Thank you for the reminder that I am to live to tell the story of the power of the Law of Attraction played out against a rich tapestry of worldly experiences."

After a sumptuous breakfast in the new hotel, I got word that I could collect my things at the Gevora. The hotel smelled of smoke, and big fans pushed a strong wind out the front door. A harried, very tired looking woman did the paperwork to get me checked out. I was given a one-day refund. A strong-legged Bhutanese man came up with me to the 41st floor on the staff-only elevator. From there, our walk up to the 48th floor went slow.

Climbing the seven floors back to my room, I kept talking to my exhausted limbs: "Come on legs." A rest stop of twelve breaths at each of the last few flights and we were there. In a rush I changed clothes and packed up my things. The Bhutanese man got my bags down quickly as I talked about the need to hurry to get to the airport. Conversation in the elevator going down revealed that the sauna on the top floor had caught on fire. It was mostly a wood fire, of all things. More thoughts about getting travel insurance.

As a general rule, do not tell an Egyptian taxi driver to drive fast! (Did I hear him softly say "Allah Akbar"?) If the fire did not kill me, this madman surely will, I thought.

But he got me to the airport on time, and the plane was on time too. Thoughts about the problems with the 737 Max dissolved when the announcer seemed to deliberately emphasize that the plane was a Boeing 780. The half-empty plane lifted easily into the air. Wheels up, I relaxed and chatted with a statuesque South African woman who worked for the American National Basketball Association. The plane was OK. I was OK. Every single thing, event, person was all super OK in the maelstrom of the full expression of the fiery Laws of the Life Force. "Bring it on!" I said out loud and smiled.

COME ON LIONS, LET'S DANCE

Arriving at my destination, I joined the others at the Phinda Private Game Reserve in Northeast South Africa, where we spent the first six days observing and participating in research activities on bird, hyenas, and elephants. On the very first day of the safari, our group of nine ended up right smack in the middle of a life and death drama: a battle between a herd of Cape buffalo and a pride of lions. It was intense! I was able to take a few pictures, but they can only suggest the ferocity of the drama we witnessed. These were very big animals intent on killing each other.

The massive Cape buffalo herd, led by a sizable dominant

female I'll call Old Mother,[5] was roaming along the south bank of the steep Dungo Ravine. The fall rains had been good to the land; the grass was a rich succulent green, knee high and more. The cows were feasting and calves nursed for long periods. A stiff wind swirled around the hills on the right side of the road and came from behind Old Mother. She did not sense that a pride of lions was hidden in the tall grass, spreading out and stalking the herd, preparing for their next kill.

A bull Cape buffalo weighing nearly a thousand pounds spotted the lions first. The outer keratin material of a Cape buffalo horn is dynamic and sluffs off due to wear or fighting; it is continuously replaced. The color tone of this enormous bull's outer horn had hints of yellow, so I named him Gold Horn. Just as our Land Cruiser slowly worked its way through the herd of Cape buffalo, Gold Horn gave chase to the first big cat he saw. Our guide, "Massi,"[6] was searching for a reported buffalo kill when we all saw the big bull chasing a lioness, who was running flat-out, the black tip of her tail bobbing in the air as she leaped through tall grass. Her run was measured. Though she gave Gold Horn the upmost respect, she instinctively knew his chase stamina was limited.

The driver pulled the Land Cruiser up close to the edge of the ravine. A small tree and some brush obscured our view, while still allowing us to see several lions in the tall grass and shrubs scattered over the surrounding area. Over the next few minutes we spotted the six members of the pride lurking in the underbrush. A deep-throated roar indicated the dominant male was down in the ravine, where despite the absence of white-back vultures circling in the air or sitting in trees to signal a kill, he was working away on the carcass of a Cape buffalo.

[5] To facilitate the narrative, I am giving names to these large and awe-inspiring creatures.
[6] Massimo Rebuzzi, one of the top-rated guides in South Africa.

The approaching herd of buffalo was a blessing to the lions. They could simply lie in wait in the brush while the herd returned to the spot, and ambush a straggler. Massi told us that this dominant male lion was old and had a distinct limp, likely from a battle with Cape buffalo.

The tension in the atmosphere was electric. It quickly became obvious that we were surrounded by lions and a very powerful Cape buffalo intent on protecting the herd. The hair on my arms stood straight up. The others in our group were equally alert. Earlier we had seen juvenile buffalo butting heads. They looked playful at first, but a pair of 400-pound animals with big sharp horns is always serious business. We'd also seen a macho juvenile buffalo confront a white rhino and bring it to a halt for almost half a minute. They stood nose to nose without moving as the rest of the herd grazed around them. The juvenile buffalo finally gave way to the much larger rhino. All in all, confrontation was in the air.

The charge of Gold Horn changed everything. According to Massi, the mighty bull knew this pride of lions well. He knew every single one of the lionesses. And then there was the gimpy king of the pride; let's call him King Gimp. He and Gold Horn were old enemies. Gold Horn had likely confronted King Gimp and the others all his life. Deep scars on his back just above the tail were reminders of what a pride of lions can do to even a thousand-pound buffalo. Since he was the dominant bull in the herd, it can be assumed that he had serviced the female whose calf was now lion lunch meat.

Massi expected Gold Horn to wreak revenge on the pride of lions if he could. He could trample a cub and sweep his massive, hooked horn into the belly of one of the big cats, tossing it in the air and eviscerating the lion or at least breaking some bones. According to Massi, King Gimp's injured leg was the outcome of a run-in with this herd of Cape buffalo, so there was no truce possible between the two groups.

Although King Gimp had recovered from his injuries, they did slow him down. Sure, he could still rush into a fray and crush the windpipe of any zebra, antelope, or buffalo brought down by the very capable female lions of his pride, but he had seen better days, and Gold Horn would trample and kill King Gimp if he got a chance. Maybe trap him in the brush or down in the ravine and gore him. Tear him apart with his hoofs and horns. Today, revenge might be his at last.

Gold Horn gave chase to Green Lady, the most powerful lioness in the pride; her impressive claws and jaws had no doubt brought down hundreds of antelope and Cape buffalo. But Green Lady eluded him, running and slumping down in the tall grass next to a small tree she could sprint behind if Gold Horn continued his pursuit. As he charged, the entire pride of lions split in every direction. A lioness I dubbed Lady Yellow ran and crouched in some tall grass on the edge of the ravine slightly above our Land Cruiser. Lady Yellow was the scout of the pride, and the hunt planner. The moment Gold Horn paused, she turned her attention to the herd of buffalo around her, seeking an opportunity to take down a disoriented calf in the confusion.

Three younger lions, the surviving subadults of Lady Yellow and Green Lady, dashed across the ravine and sank into the dense green brush, watching Gold Horn square off against the two dominant lionesses. These young lions were clearly in the relaxed repose of an audience learning the ins and outs of the death dance of lions and Cape buffalo. Their lives depended on knowing how to successfully navigate just this type of confrontation.

In a soft calm voice, Massi reassured our group, "Stay in your seats. Do not stand up. Slow movement. Splendid! Amazing! Brilliant!"

Down at the bottom of the ravine, we heard a lion roar; it was King Gimp. Gold Horn tromped and snorted and moved in a broad circle, sensing the attitude and status of each member of the pride. He knew them well. Any one of them would kill him if given half a chance. A whole pride of lions would prove a dangerous combination even for this powerful bull with his long, hooked horns and massive hoofs.

King Gimp's next roar triggered Gold Horn, who pushed the brush aside and plunged into the ravine, to where he was now directly in front of the dominant lion. From the relative safety of the Land Cruiser, we could not see King Gimp, but the antagonists had to be a mere two yards apart. The four-hundred-pound male lion, an experienced killer that had likely crushed the trachea of the buffalo he'd been feeding on (along with killing hundreds of other buffalo and antelope), faced a thousand-pound Cape buffalo ready to rush and trample him in the confines of the ravine.

Suddenly, Green Lady came out of her crouch by the big bush and darted to the edge of the ravine. Lady Yellow turned to watch but did not move from her herd-spotting position. The young lions on the opposite side of the ravine stood up as Gold Horn recognized real danger and his precarious situation. Four big lions preparing to jump on his back must have given rise to some serious life-and-death calculations.

A typical Cape buffalo fight goes something like this. A grazing buffalo becomes isolated from the herd and the lions attack. One leaps up and digs its front claws into the back of the buffalo. The buffalo surges ahead, dragging the big cat and then spinning around to try to catch the lion off balance, using his sharp, curved horns to gore and flip it high in the air. But Gold Horn realized that there was no way for him to spin around in the narrow ravine to confront the big cats. And if they jumped on his back at the same time, King Gimp would likely lunge forward and grab Gold Horn by the nose and suffocate him in minutes.

Still, even though he was face to face with Gold Horn, King Gimp did not charge. Directly behind him was a wallow of mud, and he would not be able to get any traction. Gold Horn could push him backward in a headlong charge and the bull would instantly trample him.

King Gimp stared directly into the eyes of his most fearsome enemy, and waited for backup. Then Gold Horn turned and lunged up the bank of the ravine. He charged Green Lady, who was getting ready to pounce on his back. The lioness swung around and retreated, looking over her shoulder. In the meantime, Blue Horn, another massive Cape buffalo, had come down to join Gold Horn. But they were not friends, according to Massi, having fought noisy, dusty, pitched battles for the right to mate cows in estrus. Even so, the chance to take one to the lions in tight corners was not to be missed by Blue Horn. Gold Horn and he might each get a cat!

All the while, Massi sat on the dashboard of the Land Cruiser surveying the scene. Still calm, he spoke in a measured low voice, instructing our safari members yet again not to stand up. Over and over, in a soft voice he said, "Simply brilliant!" He waxed poetic too: "This is world-class. Never before in all my years as a guide, to be this close to this kind action! This is a once in a lifetime experience."

In the Land Cruiser, we were all struck by the dramatic energy of the scene. Words seemed inadequate. "Holy shit," I heard whispered more than once. "Oh my God," someone gasped. But mostly silence, with breath held. Sheer awe. Cameras clicking. Smart phones recording. Heads turning in all directions. Where were all the big cats now? Where were the Cape buffalo? Which one was moving? Which one was ready to pounce?

Lady Yellow, the opportunity-seeking lioness, sat on her haunches eyeing the herd. Then she abruptly dropped to her belly and crouched, slowly sliding along the ground in a stalking movement toward the herd. Moments later she sat up on her haunches, again looking at the herd, only occasionally glancing back at the drama about to play out on the edge of the ravine.

Just then, two white rhinos came down the slope toward the commotion. We were now totally surrounded by lions, Cape buffalo, and white rhinos! Clearly, the rhinos were mere gawkers! But gawkers whose appearance on the scene somehow began to bring the lions and Cape buffalo back from the brink. First, the rhinos moved close to the back of the Land Cruiser, then they walked away to feed. Then Blue Horn and Gold Horn came back up the slope, and Gold Horn sensed Lady Yellow in the tall grass above our Land Cruiser. He walked directly up to the side of the Land Cruiser separating him and Lady Yellow. He stopped a foot from the vehicle. It seemed as if he intended to give Lady Yellow a cheap thrill, maybe a brief chase, but our vehicle was in the way, and he was overheated from his fracas in the ravine. Blue Horn turned and went back up the slope to the herd to eat tall green grass. Gold Horn followed.

When Lady Yellow walked down the edge of a game trail directly toward the Land Cruiser, we turned as one to watch her confident, deliberate movements. She was imposing. Maybe 250 pounds. Her paws were as big as frying pans. Initially she eyed the vehicle, before dropping her eyes to look at the ground.

Next, Lady Yellow simply walked behind the Land Cruiser and joined Green Lady. A subadult lion rolled over and played like a housecat in the tall grass near them. Mighty Cape buffalo dropped their heads to graze. Sunlight to grass, to Cape buffalo to lions to feces to fertilize the grass—all froze in place. Abruptly, the life-and-death energy-flow dance of the ages was over, for now.

Our Land Cruiser backed out of the ravine and headed back to the lodge. Later we were taken to a large pen on the edge of a plain, where two magnificent, young adult male lions were being prepared to confront King Gimp. The old boy's days were numbered. Animal carcasses were tossed into this huge cage every other day, Massi explained, cluing us in to the game reserve management plan.

Apparently, the private reserve had only one adult male lion, King Gimp, and some of the observed mating behavior was leading to inbreeding in his offspring. Thus the competition in store for him. To create new prides, these two beautiful but younger male lions would either grab off some of the stray lionesses that wandered around the reserve, or more likely, as a team, attack and kill King Gimp and supplant him. In either case, new genetic material would be entered into the lion gene pool of the reserve. The business model of hundreds of wildlife reserves includes selling surplus game such as lions, for income to other private game reserves and to try and maintain ecological balance.

During the face-off between the herd and the pride, I had my latest "Of Course" Moment. It was only natural that even on a hunting-free safari, I would find myself in the thick of a once-in-a-lifetime Cape buffalo–lion pride fight. I was elated. Elated and fully alive.

A Flood Plain of Charismatic Megafauna

In 2022, I returned to Africa for the last time, to Botswana, again on a Biologists without Borders safari, even as new waves of COVID-19 swept the planet. My legacy drama with Africa needed one more test. Immediately north of South Africa, Botswana is home to about two million people; it contains a vast expanse that seasonal rains cover with water. Rains from neighboring Angola wash down from the highlands and flood a wide breadth of the country, including the Okavango Delta, a maze of floodplains and wooded islands that is a United Nations World Heritage Site, and the home to abundant wildlife.

We spent our time in the bush where anything might happen and often does. Risks were many, notably disease, both animal- and human-inflicted (not often, but definitely possible). And although I did not experience any near-death experiences, the safari was a blast, and no easy tourist outing.

Some of us had flown in from Europe, while my travel companion Natalie and I came via Washington, D.C., and Dubai. The group met up in Johannesburg. The next day we flew to the small town of Maun in Northern Botswana, where I was pleased to see our amazing guide Massi again.

The one hour drive from Maun, along unpaved, sandy roads, to our camp on a forested island in the Delta was like the preamble to a symphony. Scattered brush villages and small herds of cattle and goats were no longer visible as we came to the double fence line marking the entrance to the protected areas. About 40 percent of the roughly 80,000 square-mile area, on the order of the size of Oregon, is under management by the Moremi Game Reserve and eighteen individual wildlife management areas.

As our group of nine, including Massi, entered the Reserve, the roadside attractions changed from cattle, goats, and donkeys to impala and zebra. Our base was adjacent to a wildlife guide training community on a shaded forest island. (A few weeks later, the water flow would turn the campsite into a true island.) We were guided to our tents and shown how to use our bathroom. The toilet was a pit with a plastic assembly to sit on. A bucket of campfire ash and a trowel set beside it. A little ash was to go into the pit after every use.

Showers found us looking up into treetops at a bucket raised by a rope, which was attached to a stand outside the tents. They took place at two p.m. daily, when the staff would bring heated water to fill the buckets. Each tent was spacious but needed to be zipped up every time we went in or out. Insects were not a problem; the concern was wildlife, especially curious baboons that we were told could make a real mess if they got in. We heard lions roar in the morning; a huge bull elephant casually walked right through the camp one afternoon. Talk about unexpected thrills!

Our days started with a wake-up call at five-thirty and a rush of coffee and cereal. By six, we were in the Land Cruiser to meet the animals moving around at dawn. After a short drive we would get out and start our walk. (This was a walking safari.) Massi loaded his rifle and we formed a line following in his exact footsteps. No joke! Exact footsteps because of snakes, aardvark holes, and thorn bushes, not to mention big game surprises—all of the foregoing were best avoided by walking in a line. We had breaks for "watering the flowers," women to the right of the Land Cruiser (because they are always right, according to our group nurse) and men to the left. One time the guys ran out of the brush zipping their pants after Massi shouted, "Lions!" A large female lion had slipped by a few trees away as the guys watered the flowers. This was the only day I was not with the group; exhausted, I had elected (or was guided?) to stay in camp.

Around eleven we would stop near a waterhole and have tea or coffee. A brick of a hard, sweetened bread-like biscuit was our staple to soak in the cup of tea. Around noon we would head back to our tent city for lunch. The African team supporting us did a fantastic job of cooking over open fires. Excellent fare for the few vegetarians in our group, too. We had warm bread with every meal cooked in a sort of Dutch oven metal box.

Then naptime and showers. Around three we gathered for short instruction on reading animal footprints in the sand, termite ecology, and bird calls. Then off for a walk in another area, at times skirting the forested islands by walking in broad circles across the dry marshlands; but not if there were Cape buffalo, hippopotamus, or lions in the general area. Once, Massi did have to "negotiate" with an overly curious bull elephant; our expert guide was always clearly very concerned about safety. Though he carried a powerful rifle on all our walking expeditions, he stated he had never needed to use it other than for target practice; he had taken first prize in a wildlife guide shooting competition.

The first night, we saw a lioness and two subadult lions stalking along the tree line of a forested island. One subadult showed early signs of a mane. We lost sight of the lioness as she slunk into deep brush near an adjacent forest island. The next morning, we found her and her two cubs. She and/or they had killed two adult warthogs, which was likely excessive for their nutritional needs, but consistent with training the subadults in hunting skills. We watched quietly from the Land Cruiser as the cubs fed on the carcasses, then lay down in the tall grass. The lioness rolled over on her back, feet in the air, her obvious round full belly advertising her comfort in that posture.

The deep-throated rumbling vocalizations of male lions in the mornings carried for over four miles, according to Massi, who also told us how a female with cubs may avoid a male, since he will attempt to kill the cubs to bring her into estrus.

On that same day a big bull elephant crashed the party. We watched him confidently move in on the feeding lions as they respectfully moved out of his way. Then he approached our Land Cruiser, huge ears flared, with a not too subtle head shake and elevated trunk. He stopped about ten feet away with his long trunk reaching out to smell us. Massi stepped out and raised his hand as a symbolic stop. He was, as he liked to say, "negotiating" with the elephant. More than one of our group was in an absolute panic. The bull stopped, then flopped his trunk over one of its long tusks. Sort of a "calm down, folks" gesture, almost humorous, a "let's talk it over, chill already" moment. Massi started the Land Cruiser engine. The noise broke the spell and the big bull turned around and sauntered back into the forest. In the back row of the Land Cruiser, my seatmates started to breathe again.

Botswana has one of the largest wild elephant populations in Africa. During the safari, we saw elephant scat and tusk marks on trees everywhere. Whole forested areas were just six feet high, with all the top branches showing the marks where they were cut off at elephant mouth height. Once, we came upon a breeding herd of about twenty-five elephants ranging in age from a few months to some maybe forty-plus-year-old females (the males are kicked out after they are about fifteen to roam as individuals or as small bachelor herds).

The herd was near a road. A large female and a juvenile male came forward, looking straight at us, shaking their heads. The male's ears flared as he stood there while the other females and smaller elephants crossed the road. In a sense, this subadult male was like a child soldier bodyguard. It was obvious that these traffic control teenagers and the lead female took their job seriously. Baby elephants are so cute! We stopped and watched for a long time.

The most abundant animals in the Okavango Delta are the impala antelope. We came across big herds that were essentially harems leading up to breeding season. A lone male would gather up to thirty females and try to keep them together, while younger or less aggressive males lingered in the background in small groups. Impala are truly beautiful with their sleek brown coat of hair and posterior markings. They are incredibly agile and on occasion we would see them bound across the open fields in long, graceful leaps.

Giraffes were less numerous. Typically, there were two to four in the same general area (not close like a herd of impala but scattered over three acres or so). We noted their special way of moving and their curiosity. Massi had a way of indirectly leading us closer to them, as if we were on a different track than directly approaching them.

The few remaining waterholes in the area were the main attractions. They were often crowded with hippos and crocodiles. Numerous big and small birds surrounded them. From about a mile away, we spotted a bull elephant ambling toward the waterhole, then wading in to drink before nonchalantly walking away, ignoring us and feeding on tall grass every few steps. Massi taught us how to read elephant tracks in the sand to determine which way they were traveling, based on the faint swish of sand at the end of the track where their toes pushed sand ahead.

We also learned to read different kinds of antelope, wild cat, hyena, zebra, and porcupine tracks. One of the most interesting finds was the impression in the sand where a leopard had laid down on its side, stretched out, and flopped its tail.

After a week in the tents, we were flown to a bit of an upscale wildlife reserve, leaving Massi behind. With new guides and new rules, our walking expeditions were severely curtailed. The guides could not have guns, only little noise-making popguns. Though venturing into the jungle on foot was discouraged, we did see some painted dogs (wild African hunting dogs) and a big monitor lizard, along with much of the same wildlife we had seen at our Maun camp. (At the upscale reserve, it was much more in our face.)

We were not allowed to go to or leave our cabins in the dark. The staff worked every morning, chasing Cape buffalo and baboons out of our resort camp before coming to get us for breakfast. The dry season grass fires filled the evening air with smoke and made for breathtaking sunsets. The fires were primarily from spontaneous combustion of dry organic matter in black soil. They started around eleven as the earth warmed up. We were all marginally affected and some in our group would not go out due to the breathing hazard.

The conclusion of the safari expedition entailed marathon travel: a small four-passenger plane from Moremi Crossing to Maun to get a COVID-19 test, and another plane to South Africa to get on an international flight. Eight hours on Emirates Air took Natalie and me to Dubai, where we had three-hour layover before boarding the fifteen-hour flight to SFO. In all, we were in fifteen airports over twenty-one days and had no health issues. It was a trip of a lifetime.

Having been in eight African countries—Nigeria, Cameroon, Dahomey, and Togo in my Nigeria years, Egypt and Morocco during my international consulting years, and now South Africa and Botswana—my only troublesome memories are of Nigeria, although Nigeria was definitely a mixed bag. Many adventures. Some of them wonderful, but a lot of bad.

I am good with Africa now, thanks, but am not likely to go back again. A bunch of other stuff is on my bucket list.

The Hunger Abides

So, after all is said and done, did my ancestors make me do it? Is my behavior in part genetically driven? If the answers are yes—and I believe they are—color me profoundly grateful. To have my wits and health intact at the age of eighty-two—if that is not cause for gratitude, I don't know what is.

When I reflect on my actions and metamorphoses, I see that there has been a quantum change, as profound as the process by which a caterpillar becomes a butterfly. But in other ways I remain essentially as I was, still drinking from the cornucopia of life: dancing, enjoying the company of women, playing golf and music. Change and growth have not so much tamed my appetite for risk as allowed me a means to channel it through other vehicles of expression.

The type of fearlessness that has been my experience from an early age is typical for children and especially young boys. They jump in the water, as I once did, without any thought of how deep the water is or how strong the current. I still recall Dad's hairy arm thrust down into the water to pull me to the surface. My brother Greg, as a career beach lifeguard, saw this jump-right-in behavior again and again.

Boys (and some girls) have to run, climb trees, throw rocks in the water. Yes, it is natural, but my conclusion is that the genetic material of children good at those activities comes from ancestors who escaped predators, while the slow runners, inept throwers, and clumsy climbers were caught before their genetic material contributed to the next generation.

❑ ❐ ❑

"Grow up!" is a phrase aimed at me from time to time. "But," I respond, "I am still Bud, an immature flower." It is not that I am afraid to grow up, it is more that growing up seems pretty boring. At times my thoughts have wandered to the concept of neoteny, the developmental retardation or retention of juvenile traits well into adulthood, to explain why fearlessness or lack of common sense is still within me. I continue to take wild runs into the breakers and swim into pounding surf. Body surfing in the volatile waters near Cabo San Lucas, Mexico, remains delightful to me. On my latest beach expedition, both my guide and colleagues confessed to having considered the impossibility of retrieving my body if I drowned. But here I am!

As noted throughout, genetic combinations are likely at play in my approach to life. By now, scientists know some things about the set of genes that predisposes people to fear or the lack of it. In fact, studies on twins and triplets separated at birth powerfully, sometimes disconcertingly, suggest that we really need to rethink the whole binary nature/nurture divide. Though we are obviously not as fixed in our behavior as a caterpillar, *aspects* of our behavior certainly are fixed in our inherited DNA. Authors David Buss and Steven Pinker, both highly recommended, have influenced my thoughts on the subject.

To further complicate matters, DNA can be *shaped*, and consequently both the brain and behavior can be modified. Meaning that my survival in potentially fatal situations likely modified the expression of those genes to potentiate even more risky future adventures.

This is where my recommendations to parents come in. Treat your kids to the most challenging and diverse set of experiences possible. They need to learn to adapt to the tectonic shift in our global socioeconomic and environmental culture. Go places with them, including other countries, often. Do not plan everything out. Send them to adventure or leadership training classes. Learn foreign languages and teach them to your kids. Treat their cuts and bumps as normal. The human genome requires adaptive survival skills. Our future relatives will applaud you!

Then there are alternative spiritual explanations: maybe a higher energy form, a sentient but invisible Life Force, dictates the venues and players of life's trajectories. Are we just transitory life forms on the surface of this planet, no more or less significant than a blade of grass? Leaves on a sort of deciduous Tree of Life. Is there any way to really know, given the limitations of our intellectual and scientific tools in the early years of the twenty-first century? Or was I just a one real lucky nut case?

To dispel the "Lucky Crazy Guy" theory, I recently filled out the Sixteen Personality Factor Questionnaire (16PF) and was found to fall into the normal range for most factors, but with particularly strong tendencies in "warmth" to other people, "openness to change," and "emotional stability." My lowest levels were "rule-consciousness" and "privateness." None of this surprised me.

Many years ago I was advised to meet with a psychiatrist to see if I was manic-depressive. (At least one member of my extended family is certified as such.) After three meetings, the shrink determined that I was high energy, and instructed me to get enough sleep during the workweek so that I didn't sleep all weekend and make family members keep checking in to see if I had "turned blue yet." Good advice!

The question of genetic drivers is still open, but my investigation continues. I have reached out to several genetic consulting groups to find out if the DNA alleles for fear or lack of fear show up in my genetic profile.

Meanwhile, I stand by my considered belief that the human genome has a built-in instruction manual for producing a range of individual types, some of which are programed to take on risks to test the environment. The genome appears to want some individuals with curiosity, to try things most of us do not want or know how to do. My own genetic tool chest must contain a set of instructions predisposing me to be the type that gets creative and builds a raft, to paddle across a crocodile-infested river to reach an abundance of food, while others in the tribe watch and hope.

"THE BRIDGE IS BROKEN, YOU CANNOT LEAVE"

My latest adventure took place in Costa Rica, where severe weather blocked off the only road out of Limón. A substantial earthquake centered ninety miles away in Nicaragua was the inciting incident. This all took place just as Kathryn, my platonic travel companion, and I were completing a scouting trip to pick a site for our first Lighten Up! Spiritual Retreat

After a week on the Pacific coast, where we were charmed by Playa Hermosa, we'd been preparing to fly home. But first we wanted to check out the Caribbean, windward side of the country. Traveling there, we found a small lovely hotel on the beach, and were resting and enjoying the Caribbean surf, and chatting with locals about our mission. We also visited an indigenous community farm and watched as they made cocoa powder the traditional way, using heavy rocks to crush the seeds.

Then, as we were sipping fresh cocoa, the hut trembled and its support post swayed side to side. We dashed out and held onto trees. It was a serious jolt! But earthquakes are not unusual in that part of the world, where volcanic seismic activity is common. Nervous laughter followed, but Kathryn gave me a sidelong look. She'd heard how unusual and precarious events follow me everywhere I go.

Then the wall of rain arrived. Followed by knock-you-right-out-of-your-bed screaming thunder and lightning directly over the hotel. Next came sheets of rain night and day. About thirty-six hours of some of the most torrential rain I have ever seen—and I have spent decades in remote parts of the world and seen plenty of downpours. Lately though, the warming of the planet and oceans has resulted in ever-increasing evaporation; consequently, downpours and flooding are becoming almost routine. Meteorologically, it is nothing more than the dumping of moisture in the air back to earth.

This went on and on, stranding us. The sun was blacked out. Day was like evening. The hotel courtyard flooded. Hotel beach furniture was ripped up and blown over. And worst of all, a large river had overflowed its banks, topping the deck of the one bridge out of town, a regional disaster, especially for Puerto Limón, which is a major freight terminal and also a tourist center.

When it seemed we were going to miss our flight home, we priced hiring a helicopter that could land on a local soccer field—but at three thousand dollars apiece that was a no-go. Besides, Kathryn said she could not possibly get inebriated enough to get into a helicopter on a wet soccer field and take off in lousy weather.

Then a backpacker told us we could chance walking across a finger of road that remained on the edge of the bridge. Kathryn and I conferred, and decided to take the risk. So we rode by taxi to the river, where torrential rains had eroded the river's banks, washing out most of the bridge footing and weakening what was left of it. The earthquake must have further weakened the bridge. There was a huge hole in the middle, but a narrow paved section remained.

We carefully pulled our roller suitcases across the small section of the bridge, even as another section collapsed behind us. We then made our way home without further incident. Kathryn was a bit tight-lipped, but I reminded her that this was well within the range of experiences that follow me and that I always make it out OK and so do the people with me.

My appetite is still there. The risks continue to find me and vice versa. I consider it my biological duty to live to the Life Force's full expression, and to be an exemplar, so others can come to know how to survive an increasingly challenging world. Bridges may collapse, but I will walk across anyway. Cryptocurrency and other financial instruments will boom and bust, but fortune favors the brave, and I have done well enough to finance a comfortable lifestyle and continue to seek out adventures others wouldn't have even if you paid them.

Kathryn and I went ahead and booked the lovely spot in Playa Hermosa along the peaceful Pacific coast for our first retreat. What could possibly go wrong?

BUD'S 2022 LIFE EXTENSION PLAN
FOR 105+ YEARS OLD IN EXCELLENT HEALTH

The following list is my reminder to ensure that I keep living long enough to do more, to keep having adventures. It is taped to my refrigerator door, as a challenge to my biological clock.

HAVE FUN: Laugh, tell jokes, smile, make love, play!

SLEEP: 8 hrs. per night. One or two short naps per day

EXERCISE: 60 min. per day*

MEDITATE: 20 to 30 min. per day. Go deep on OM, *Transformation*, Vipassana

FOOD INTAKE: Minimize sugar, more vegetables, eat with others

CONSUMPTION: Intermittent fasting (one day per month). Weight target 190 lbs.

HEALTH: Schedule and keep medical appointments

PRESCRIPTIONS: Testosterone cream, sildenafil, Pradaxa

SUPPLEMENTS: Nicotinamide riboside, Resveratrol, D3, NO

INFRARED LIGHT: Twice a week, morning & afternoon light exposure

HYPERBARIC OXYGEN TREATMENT: Twice a month

STUDY: Astronomy, brain function, telomeres, great literature

MUSIC: Jam with others twice a week. Write and record 4 new songs a year

DANCE: Go dancing at least twice per month, take dance classes

RELATIONSHIPS: Develop new interpersonal relationships

TRAVEL: Six travel adventures per year

NEWS: Read and watch less!

BUSINESS: Invest in growth and innovations

WRITING: Finish AFR (this book) Learn how to market books. Write *Transformation II*

PUBLICATIONS: Write articles for publication, kindness, and truth

PUBLIC SPEAKING: Two+ public speaking engagements per year

BRAIN STIMULATION: Direct Current brain stimulation, binaural beats

PSYCHIC PHENOMENA: Controlled Remote Viewing, astral travel, energy forms

SPIRITUAL JOURNEY: Ask for guidance, practice abiding non-duality, awareness

HAVE MORE FUN: Deliciously enjoy every moment

I should note that when it comes to health aids, my approach is to do my research, and not to ignore the mandatory recitation of side effects which is the bane of evening TV watching. Then, in the spirit of venturesome curiosity, where the potential rewards substantially outweigh the downside, I plunge in.

*Exercise has always been part of my life: strength workouts, swimming, golf, and bicycling (but less so after a bike accident when I was sixty-nine that nearly killed me and destroyed the ligaments in my shoulder). At seventy, I was ranked 125th nationally for my age by the American Triathlon Association. To this day, there is a chin-up bar next to my bed and I keep rubber power cords in the bathroom to get a brief muscle exercise almost every morning.

SOURCES / INSPIRATION

C. L. Apicella, A. N. Crittenden, V. A. Tobolsky. "Hunter-Gatherer Males Are More Risk-Seeking than Females, Even in Late Childhood." *Evolution and Human Behavior* 38(5):592–603. September 2017.

Susan Block. *The Bonobo Way: The Evolution of Peace through Pleasure.* Gardner & Daughters. 2014.

Hari Chitan. *The Bhagavad Gita Summarized and Simplified: A Comprehensive and Easy-to-Read Summary of the Divine Song of God.* The Bhagavad Gita Series. Independently published. 2021.

William R. Clark. "Is Our Tendency to Experience Fear and Anxiety Genetic?" *Scientific American.* March 6, 2000.

Jared Diamond. *The Third Chimpanzee: The Evolution and Future of the Human Animal.* Harper Collins. 1991.

The Gospel According to Thomas (II 2). The Nag Hammadi Library. 117–130. Harper and Row. 1977.

Yuval Noah Harari. *Sapiens: A Brief History of Humankind.* Harper. 2015.

Christopher Intagliata. "Brain Scan Might Reveal Appetite for Risk." *Scientific American.* April 6, 2018.

Wi Hoon Jung, Sangil Lee, Caryn Lerman, Joseph W. Kable. "Amygdala Functional and Structural Connectivity Predicts Individual Risk Tolerance." *Neuron* 98(2):394–404. April 18, 2018.

Tula Karras. "Your Emotions: The Science of How You Feel." *National Geographic.* January 17, 2020.

J. Petraitis, C. Lampman, R. Boeckmann, E. Falconer. "Sex Differences in the Attractiveness of Hunter-Gatherer and Modern Risk." *Journal of Applied Social Psychology*. June 1, 2014.

David Reich. *Who We Are and How We Got There: Ancient DNA and the New Science of the Human Past*. Vintage. 2019.

Jane Roberts. *The Nature of Personal Reality: A Seth Book*. Prentice Hall. 1974.

Christopher Ryan and Cacilda Jetha. *Sex at Dawn: The Prehistoric Origins of Modern Sexuality*. HarperCollins. 2010.

Helen Schucman and William Thetford. *A Course in Miracles*. Foundation for Inner Peace. 1976.

Karen B. Strier and Don Brenneis. "Introduction: Risk and Knowledge." *Annual Review of Anthropology* 43. 2014.

ACKNOWLEDGMENTS

Thanks to some wonderful friends and amazing family members, this set of stories and speculations from the overlapping parts of my life as a scientist and a seeker has become the book I'd hoped it would it.

The Abbott clan—Greg, Susanna, Linda, Celia, Germania, Tom, Michelle, Zeph, Marcia, and Cynthia—had a few laughs, comments, and corrections, while generally appreciating reading my version of what the hell actually happened. I would also like to thank my magnificent, loving, and generous parents, whom you've met in the book.

Patricia Stevens and Dorothy Herzberg validated my Nigerian adventures. Steven Burley and Gordy Fowler taught me how to fish in Hawaiian waters. Both of them had a few laughs and raised eyebrows about some of my fish stories. Hey! They're fish stories!

Natalie Nussbaum was there for many adventures, especially in Botswana and explorations in consciousness. Rusty Gill, Brian Sedgwick, Jean Tang, Robert Coats, Paula Croskey, Christiana Tran, and Jeanne McGuire were eager readers who gave me valuable feedback. Mostly, though, I suspect they were mostly glad to get to know me in my historical context compared to how they know me now.

Thanks to Jennifer Powers for helping develop a theme and to Dr. Hank Segal for the psychological test.

Priscila Soares and Kathryn Remati, my two talented partners in the ongoing Lighten Up Retreats and other travels in

Latin America, posed a few awkward follow-up questions relating to whether I actually had changed my far less than Politically Correct (PC) behavior patterns and words. Priscila is also the hand behind the cover art.

Mark Weiman of Regent Press came along late in the game, but just in time to coordinate the finalization of this book, including typesetting and design.

Finally, without overstating it, this book would not have been possible to finish without my tireless and patient editor and "book shepherd" Kurt Lipschutz.

ABOUT THE AUTHOR

ROBERT R. ABBOTT was born in 1941 and raised in San Diego, California. He is a practicing marine biologist with a PhD from the University of Washington. Before remaking himself into a writer for the wider public, he authored numerous scientific publications and technical reports. (At 82, he remains active as a consulting marine biologist and expert witness.) In 2021, he published his first book (written with Zochi Young), *TRANSFORMATION: The 90-Second Mind-Body Practice Integrating Tai Chi and Yoga to Manage Stress and Unlock Your Potential.* He is a co-leader of the Lighten Up Retreats organization, and an advisor and trainer on what it takes to live fully to a ripe old age.

Appetite for Risk ties the dramatic experiences of his life in with digressions on the forces that have contributed to his survival. It combines the perspectives of genetic drivers (DNA), nurturing strategies, and spiritual linkages, looking back in time and generations to reveal the behavior of his ancestors as expressed in his own attitudes and actions. His advice to parents is to present numerous challenges to their children to better enable them to face and adapt to the changes inherent in our rapidly evolving global social-economic environment.